nickelodeon

降去神通
AVATAR
THE LAST AIRBENDER™

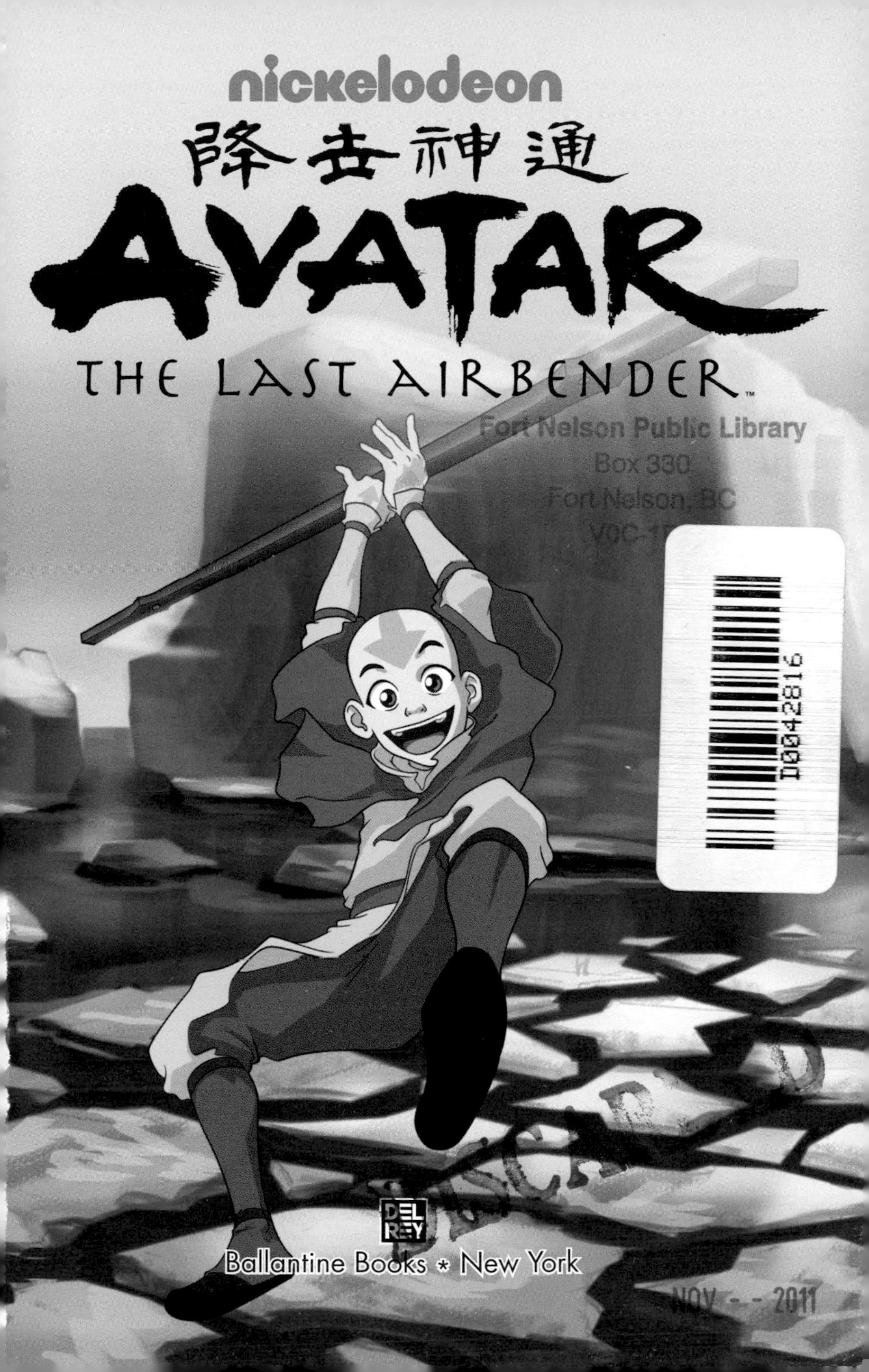

DEL REY

Ballantine Books * New York

A Del Rey Manga Trade Paperback Edition

Published in the United States by Del Rey, an imprint of The Random House Publishing Group, a division of Random House, Inc., New York.

DEL REY is a registered trademark and the Del Rey colophon is a trademark of Random House, Inc.

Originally published in 2006 by TokyoPop.

ISBN 978-0-345-51853-8

Printed in the United States of America on acid-free paper

www.delreymanga.com

9 8 7 6 5 4 3 2 1

降去神通

AVATAR

THE LAST AIRBENDER™

Created by
Michael Dante DiMartino
& Bryan Konietzko

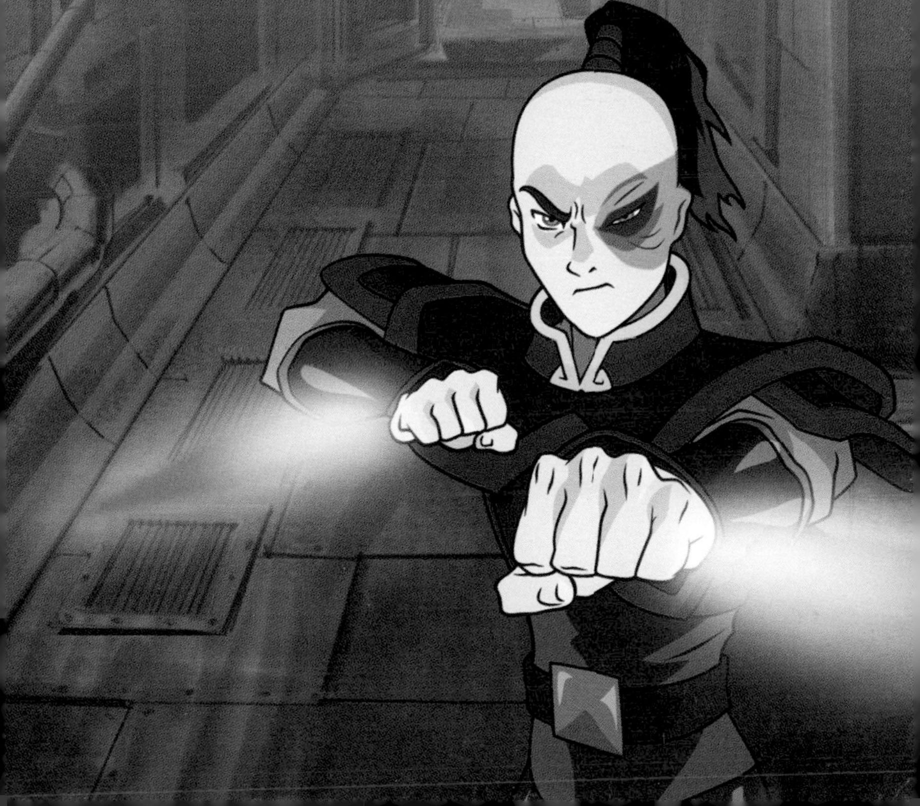

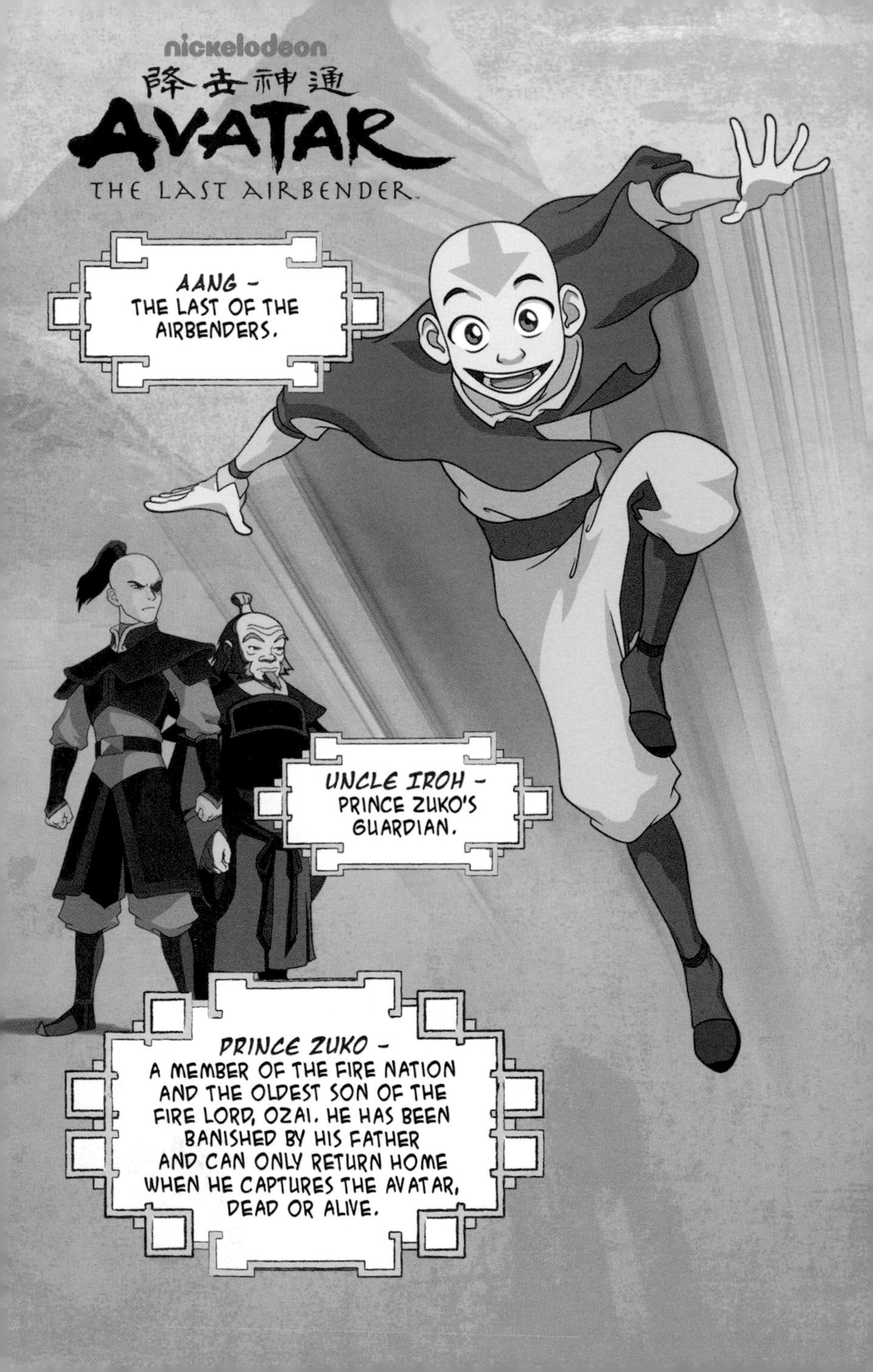
nickelodeon
降去神通
AVATAR
THE LAST AIRBENDER
AANG - THE LAST OF THE AIRBENDERS.
UNCLE IROH - PRINCE ZUKO'S GUARDIAN.
PRINCE ZUKO - A MEMBER OF THE FIRE NATION AND THE OLDEST SON OF THE FIRE LORD, OZAI. HE HAS BEEN BANISHED BY HIS FATHER AND CAN ONLY RETURN HOME WHEN HE CAPTURES THE AVATAR, DEAD OR ALIVE.

THE STORY SO FAR...

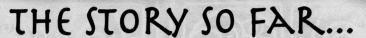

WHILE OUT FISHING, KATARA AND HER BROTHER SOKKA DISCOVER A YOUNG BOY CALLED AANG AND HIS FLYING BISON, APPA, TRAPPED IN AN ICEBERG. BREAKING HIM OUT OF HIS FROZEN PRISON, THEY LEARN THAT HE IS AN AIRBENDER AND HAS BEEN TRAPPED IN THE ICE FOR A HUNDRED YEARS.

THE GROUP RETURNS TO THE WATER TRIBE'S VILLAGE, NOT KNOWING THAT FREEING AANG HAS ALERTED A FIRE NAVY WARSHIP CARRYING THE TERRIBLE PRINCE ZUKO.

NOW PRINCE ZUKO KNOWS THE SECRET LOCATION OF THE WATER VILLAGE AND IS ON HIS WAY TO DESTROY IT. WILL SOKKA, KATARA, AND AANG FIND OUT IN TIME TO SAVE THE VILLAGE?

THE AVATAR RETURNS

WRITTEN BY
MICHAEL DANTE DIMARTINO
& BRYAN KONIETZKO

ADDITIONAL WRITING BY
AARON EHASZ, PETER GOLDFINGER,
AND JOSH STOLBERG

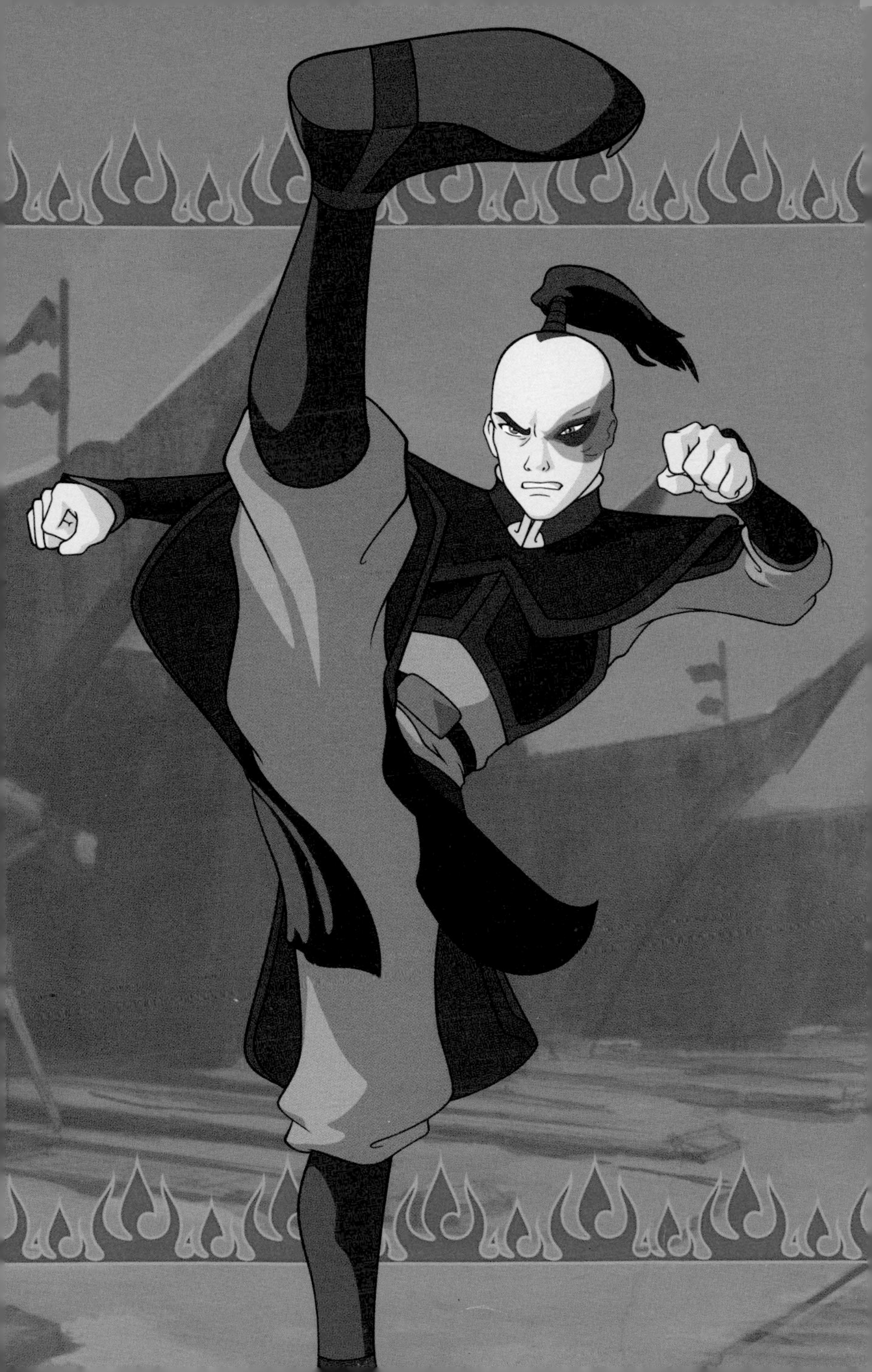

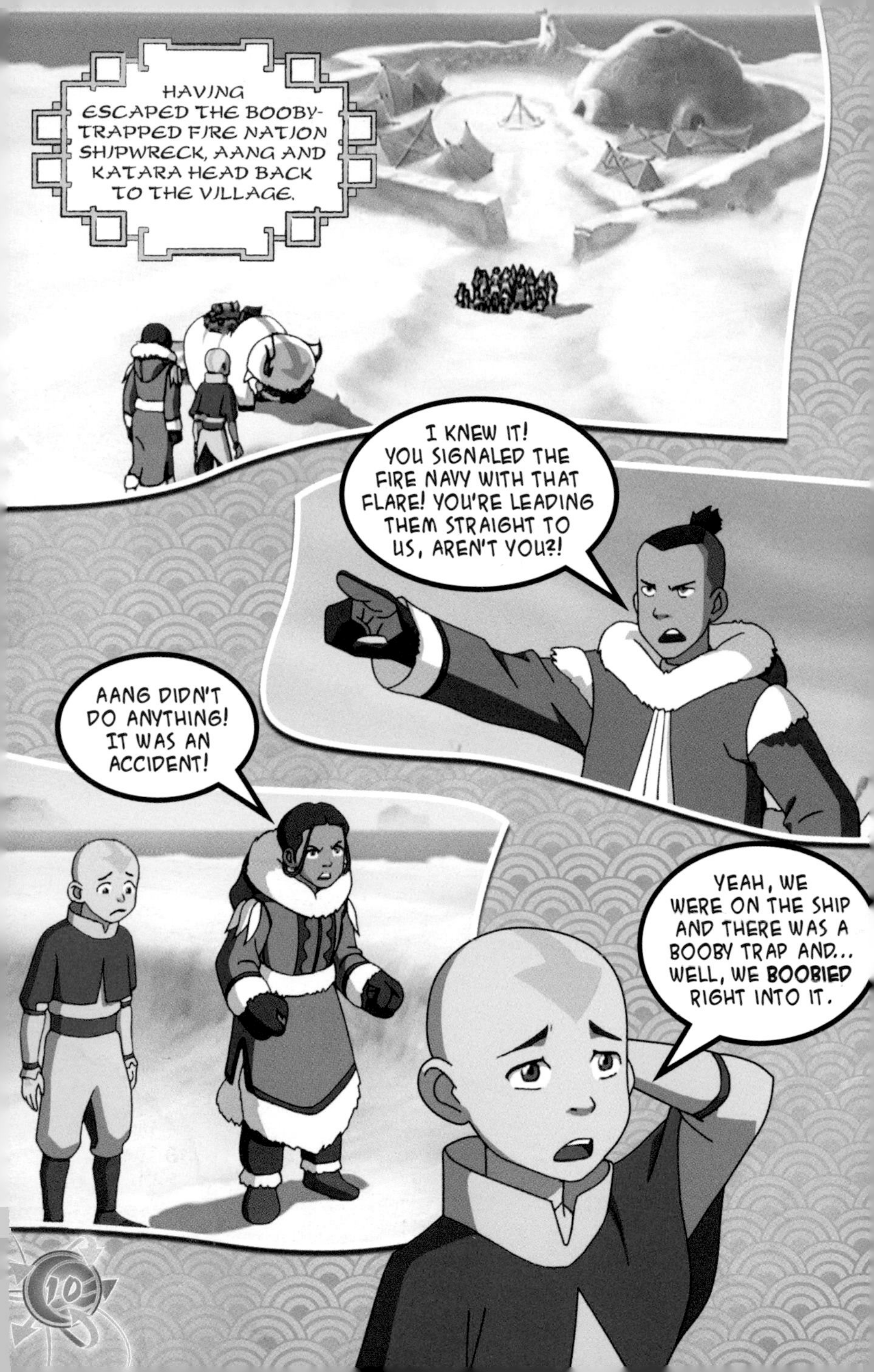
HAVING ESCAPED THE BOOBY-TRAPPED FIRE NATION SHIPWRECK, AANG AND KATARA HEAD BACK TO THE VILLAGE.
I KNEW IT! YOU SIGNALED THE FIRE NAVY WITH THAT FLARE! YOU'RE LEADING THEM STRAIGHT TO US, AREN'T YOU?!
AANG DIDN'T DO ANYTHING! IT WAS AN ACCIDENT!
YEAH, WE WERE ON THE SHIP AND THERE WAS A BOOBY TRAP AND... WELL, WE **BOOBIED** RIGHT INTO IT.

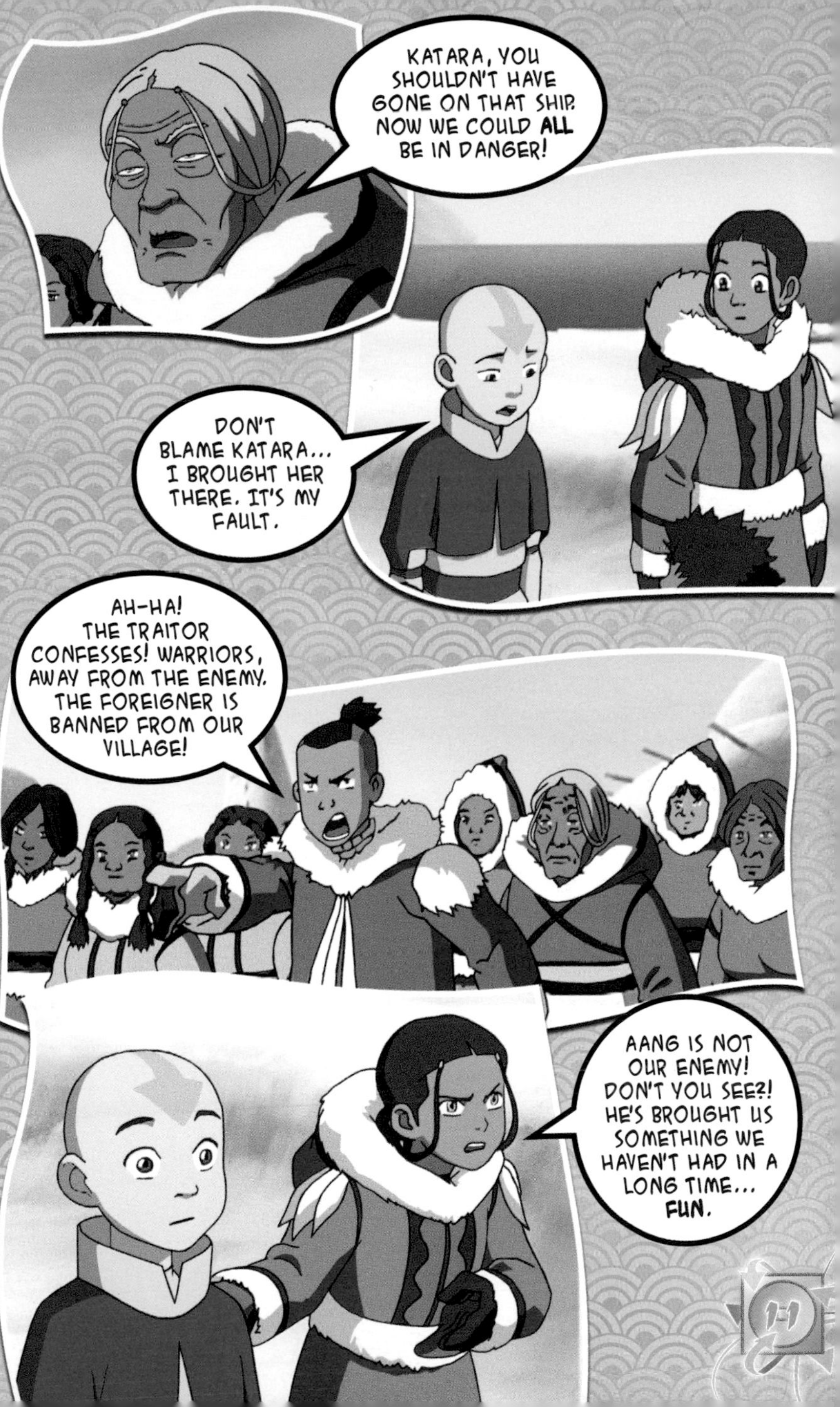
KATARA, YOU SHOULDN'T HAVE GONE ON THAT SHIP. NOW WE COULD ALL BE IN DANGER!
DON'T BLAME KATARA... I BROUGHT HER THERE. IT'S MY FAULT.
AH-HA! THE TRAITOR CONFESSES! WARRIORS, AWAY FROM THE ENEMY. THE FOREIGNER IS BANNED FROM OUR VILLAGE!
AANG IS NOT OUR ENEMY! DON'T YOU SEE?! HE'S BROUGHT US SOMETHING WE HAVEN'T HAD IN A LONG TIME... FUN.

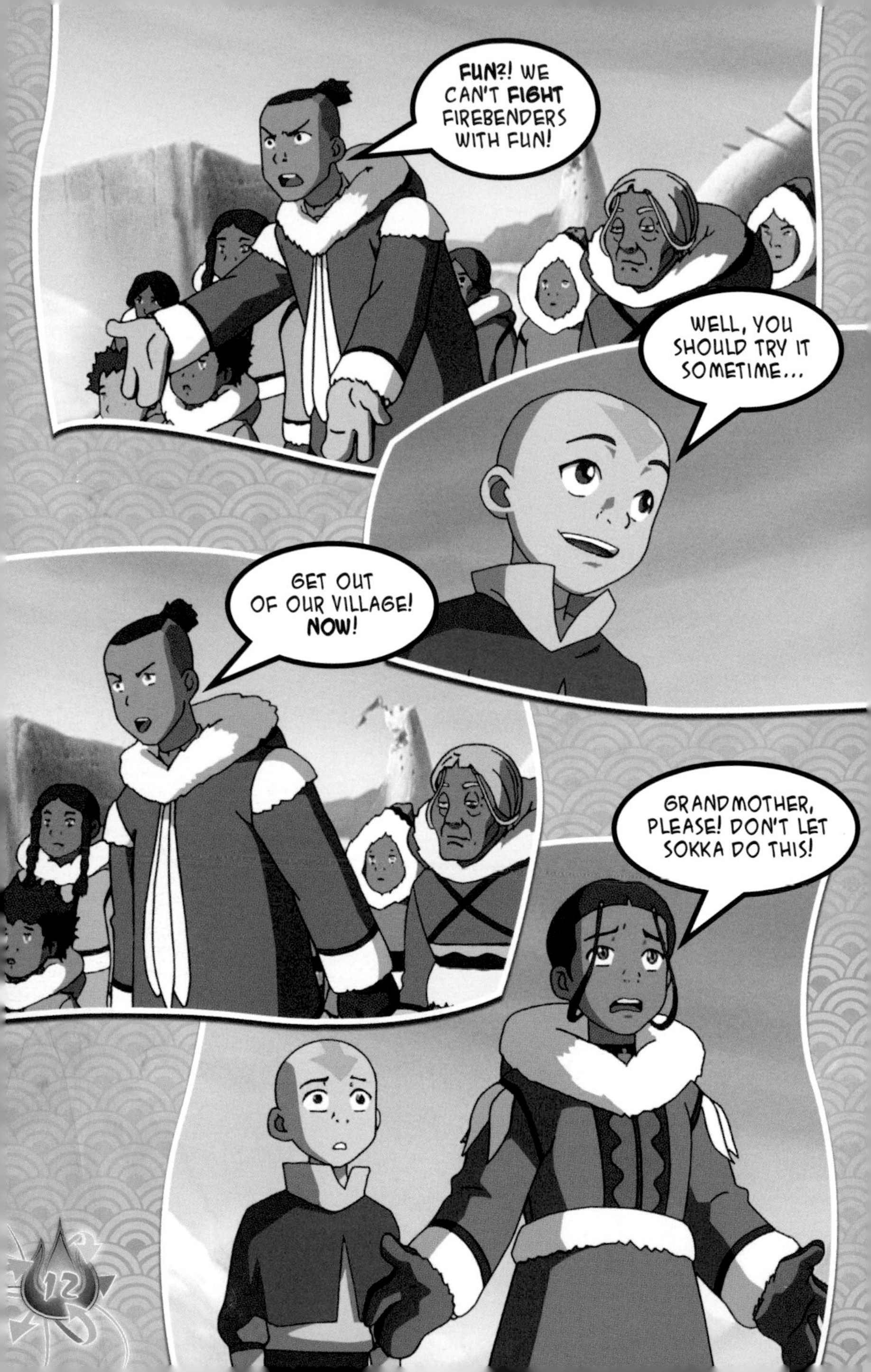
FUN?! WE CAN'T FIGHT FIREBENDERS WITH FUN!
WELL, YOU SHOULD TRY IT SOMETIME...
GET OUT OF OUR VILLAGE! NOW!
GRANDMOTHER, PLEASE! DON'T LET SOKKA DO THIS!

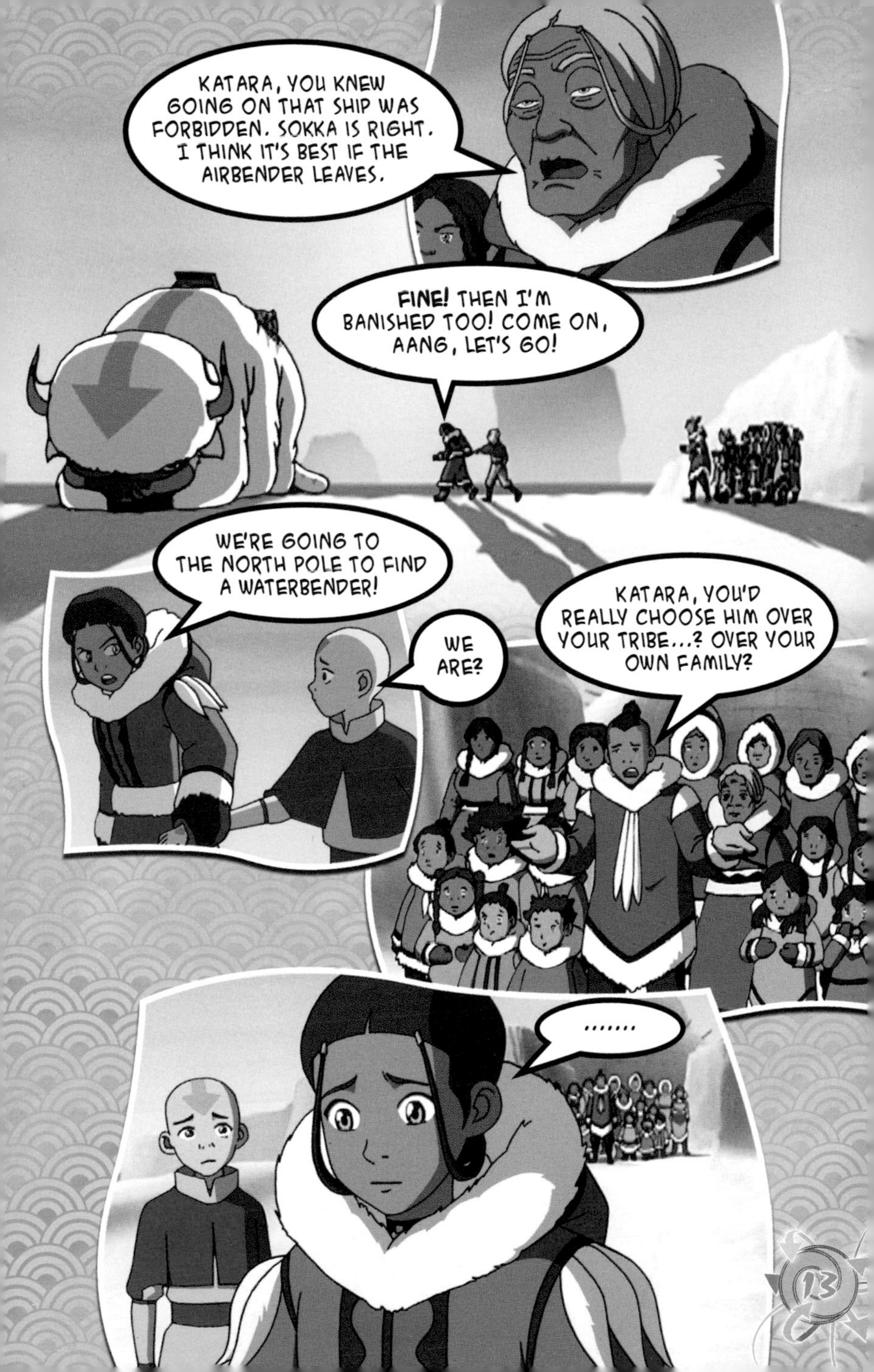
KATARA, YOU KNEW GOING ON THAT SHIP WAS FORBIDDEN. SOKKA IS RIGHT. I THINK IT'S BEST IF THE AIRBENDER LEAVES.
FINE! THEN I'M BANISHED TOO! COME ON, AANG, LET'S GO!
WE'RE GOING TO THE NORTH POLE TO FIND A WATERBENDER!
WE ARE?
KATARA, YOU'D REALLY CHOOSE HIM OVER YOUR TRIBE...? OVER YOUR OWN FAMILY?
....

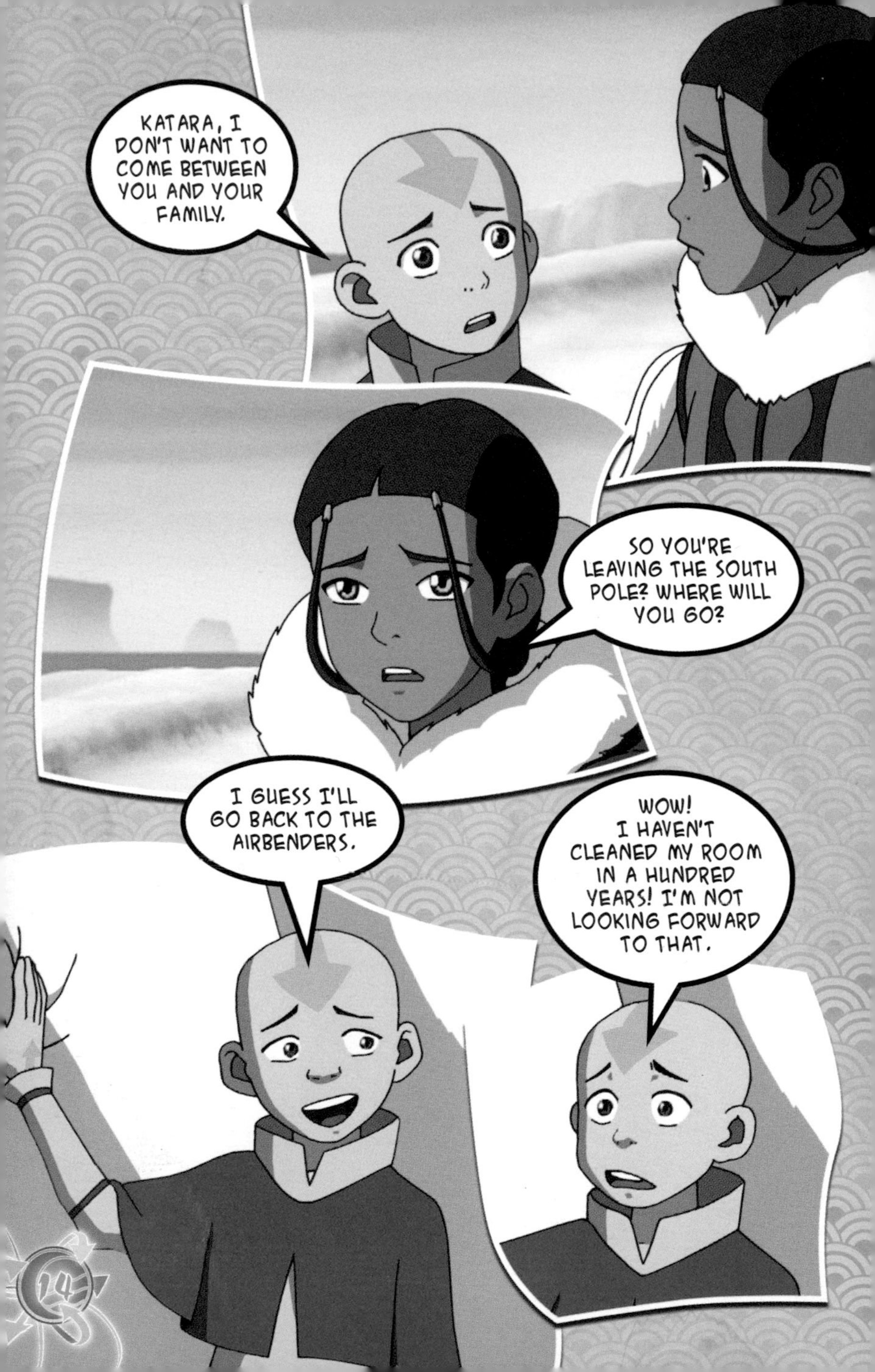
KATARA, I DON'T WANT TO COME BETWEEN YOU AND YOUR FAMILY.
SO YOU'RE LEAVING THE SOUTH POLE? WHERE WILL YOU GO?
I GUESS I'LL GO BACK TO THE AIRBENDERS.
WOW! I HAVEN'T CLEANED MY ROOM IN A HUNDRED YEARS! I'M NOT LOOKING FORWARD TO THAT.

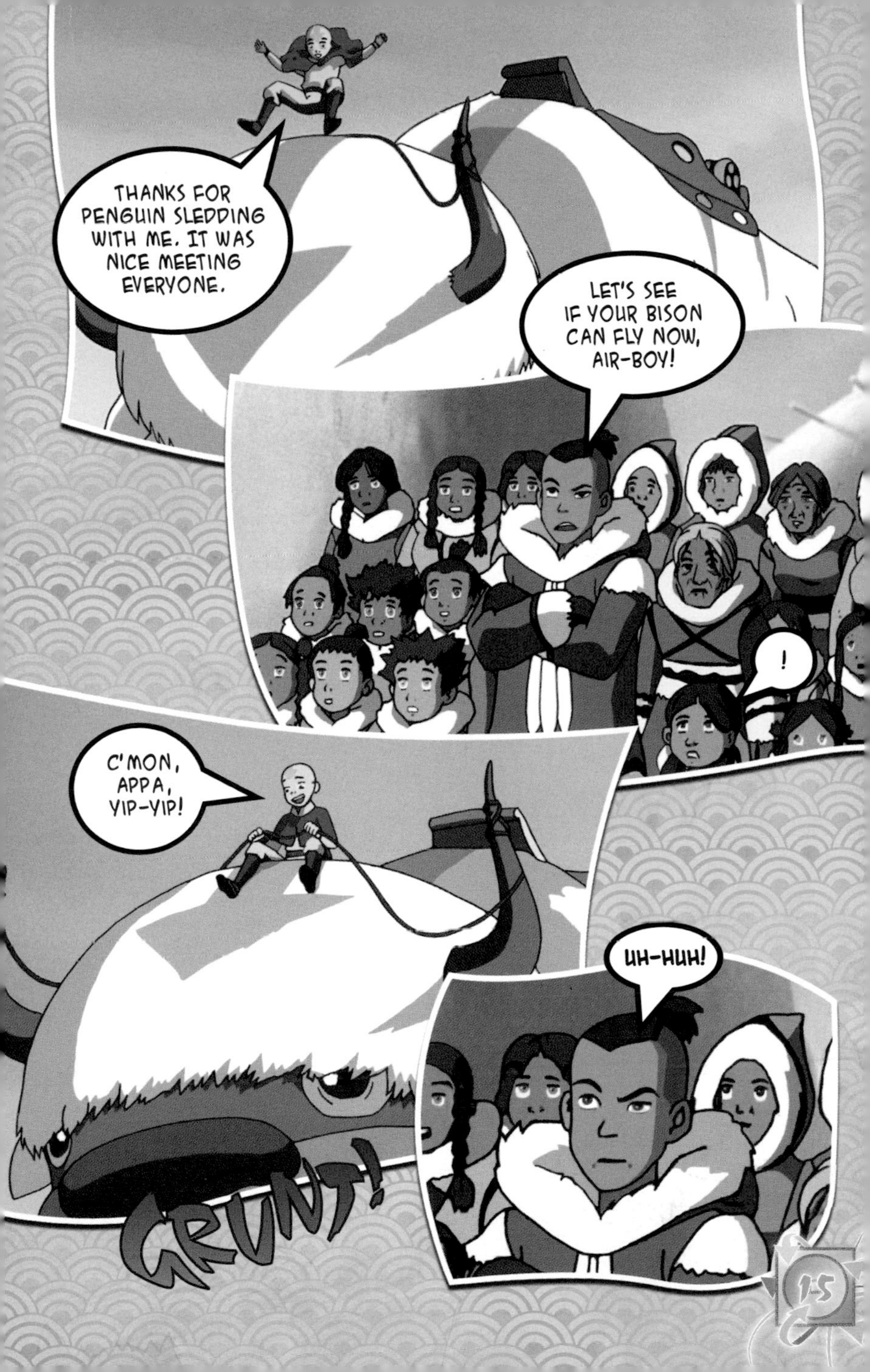
THANKS FOR PENGUIN SLEDDING WITH ME. IT WAS NICE MEETING EVERYONE.
LET'S SEE IF YOUR BISON CAN FLY NOW, AIR-BOY!
!
C'MON, APPA, YIP-YIP!
GRUNT!
UH-HUH!

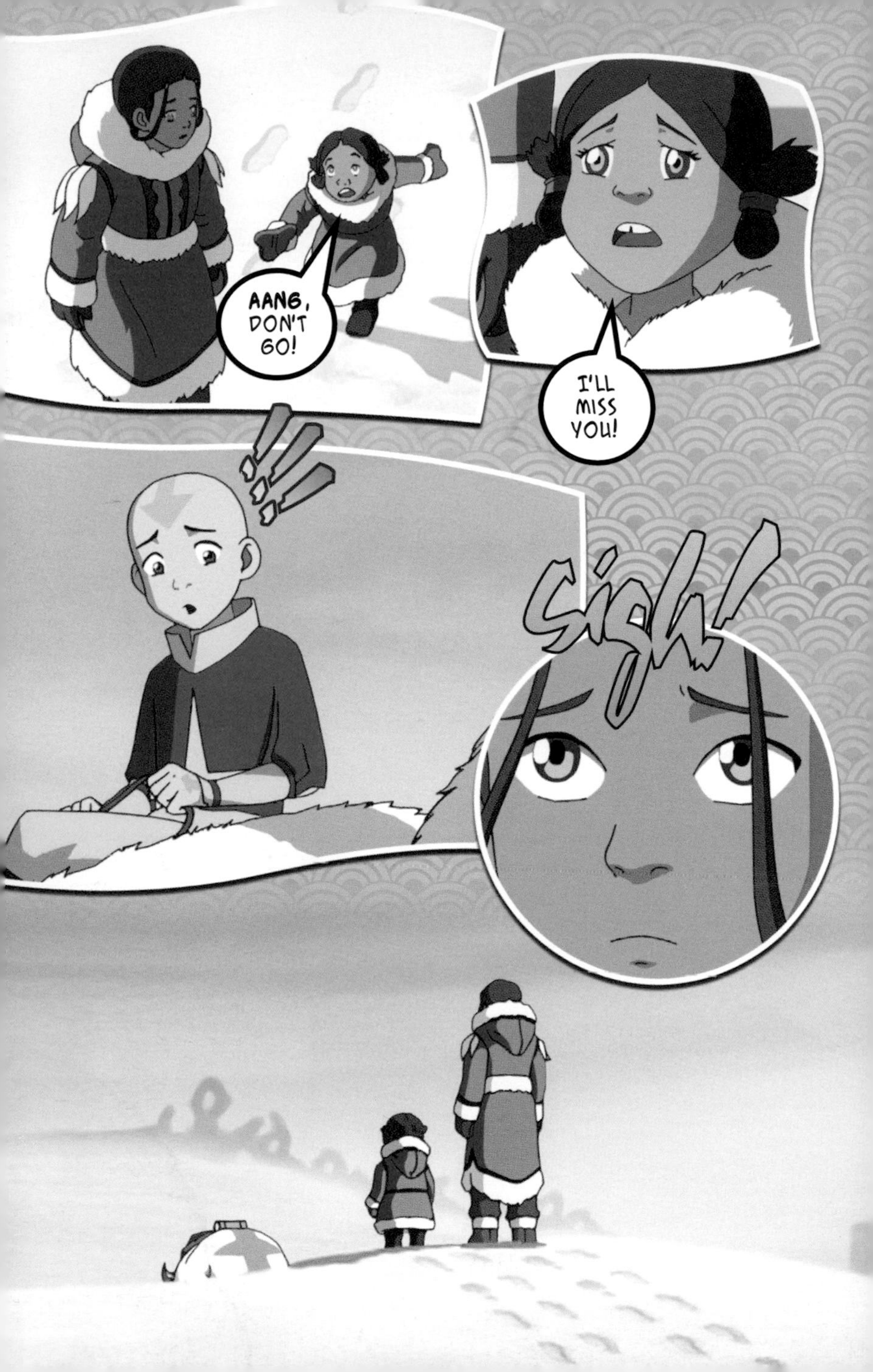
AANG, DON'T GO!
I'LL MISS YOU!
SIGH!

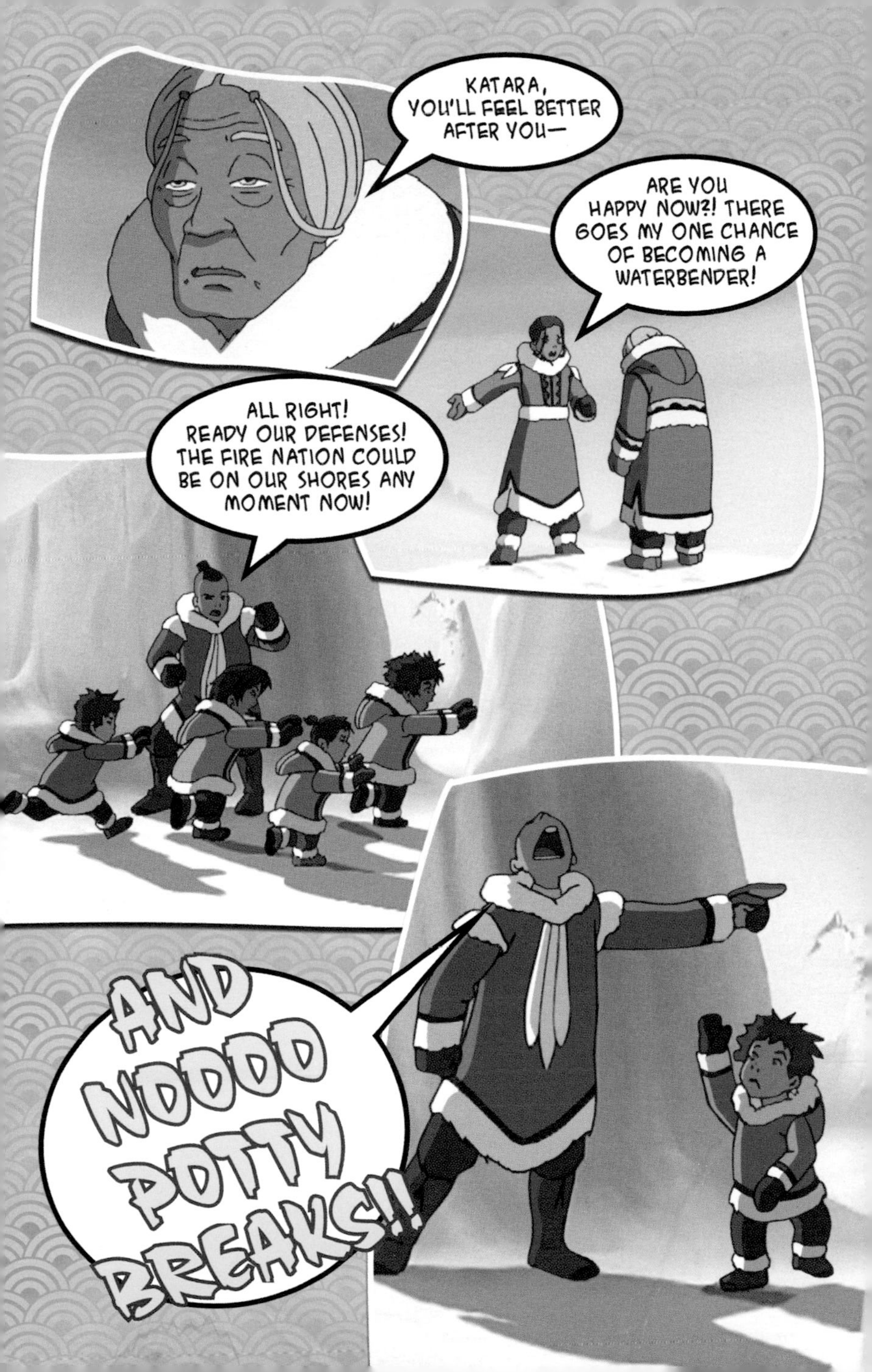
KATARA, YOU'LL FEEL BETTER AFTER YOU—
ARE YOU HAPPY NOW?! THERE GOES MY ONE CHANCE OF BECOMING A WATERBENDER!
ALL RIGHT! READY OUR DEFENSES! THE FIRE NATION COULD BE ON OUR SHORES ANY MOMENT NOW!
AND NOOOO POTTY BREAKS!!

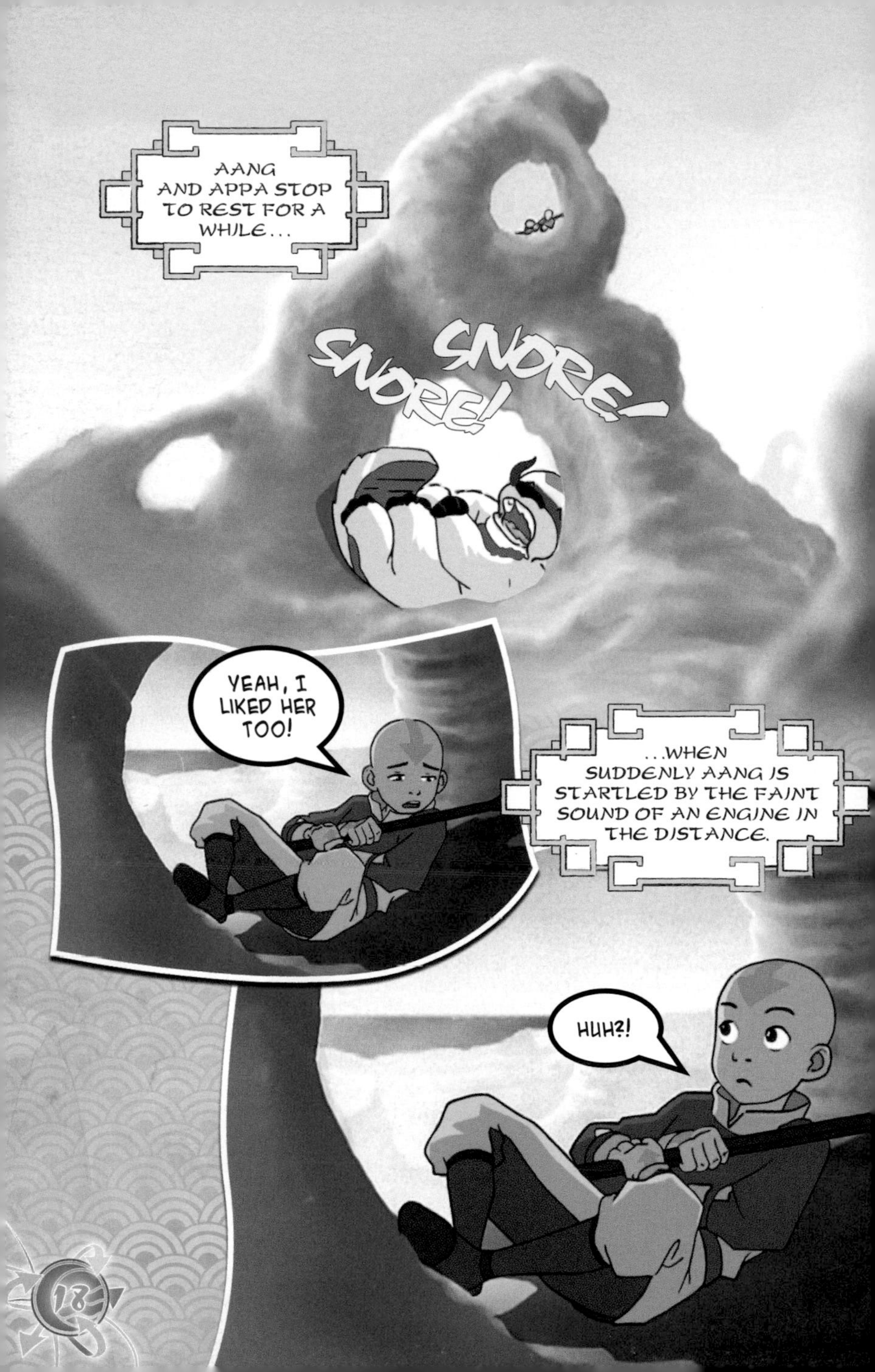
AANG AND APPA STOP TO REST FOR A WHILE . . .
SNORE!
SNORE!
YEAH, I LIKED HER TOO!
. . .WHEN SUDDENLY AANG IS STARTLED BY THE FAINT SOUND OF AN ENGINE IN THE DISTANCE.
HUH?!

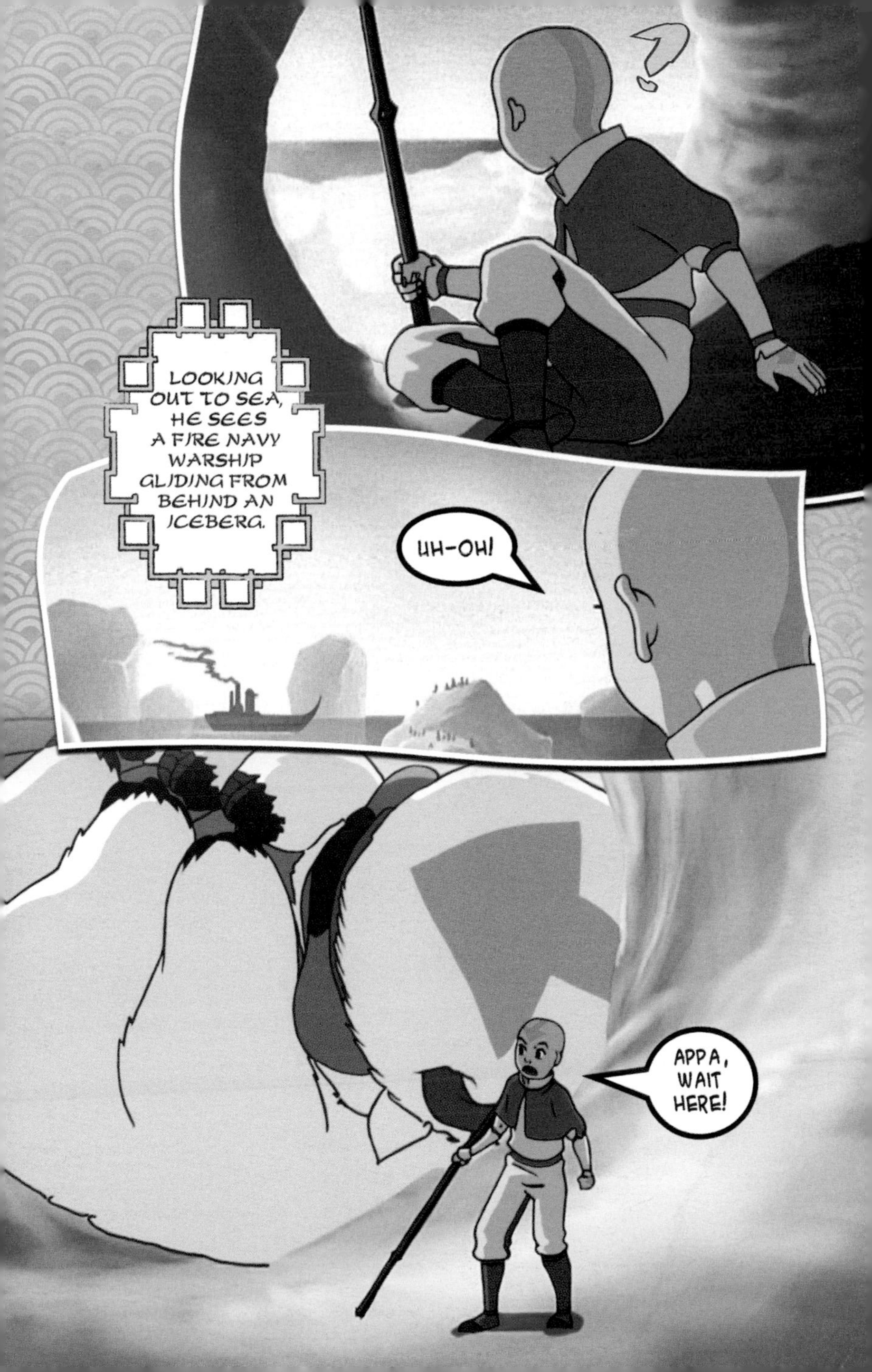
LOOKING OUT TO SEA, HE SEES A FIRE NAVY WARSHIP GLIDING FROM BEHIND AN ICEBERG.
UH-OH!
APPA, WAIT HERE!

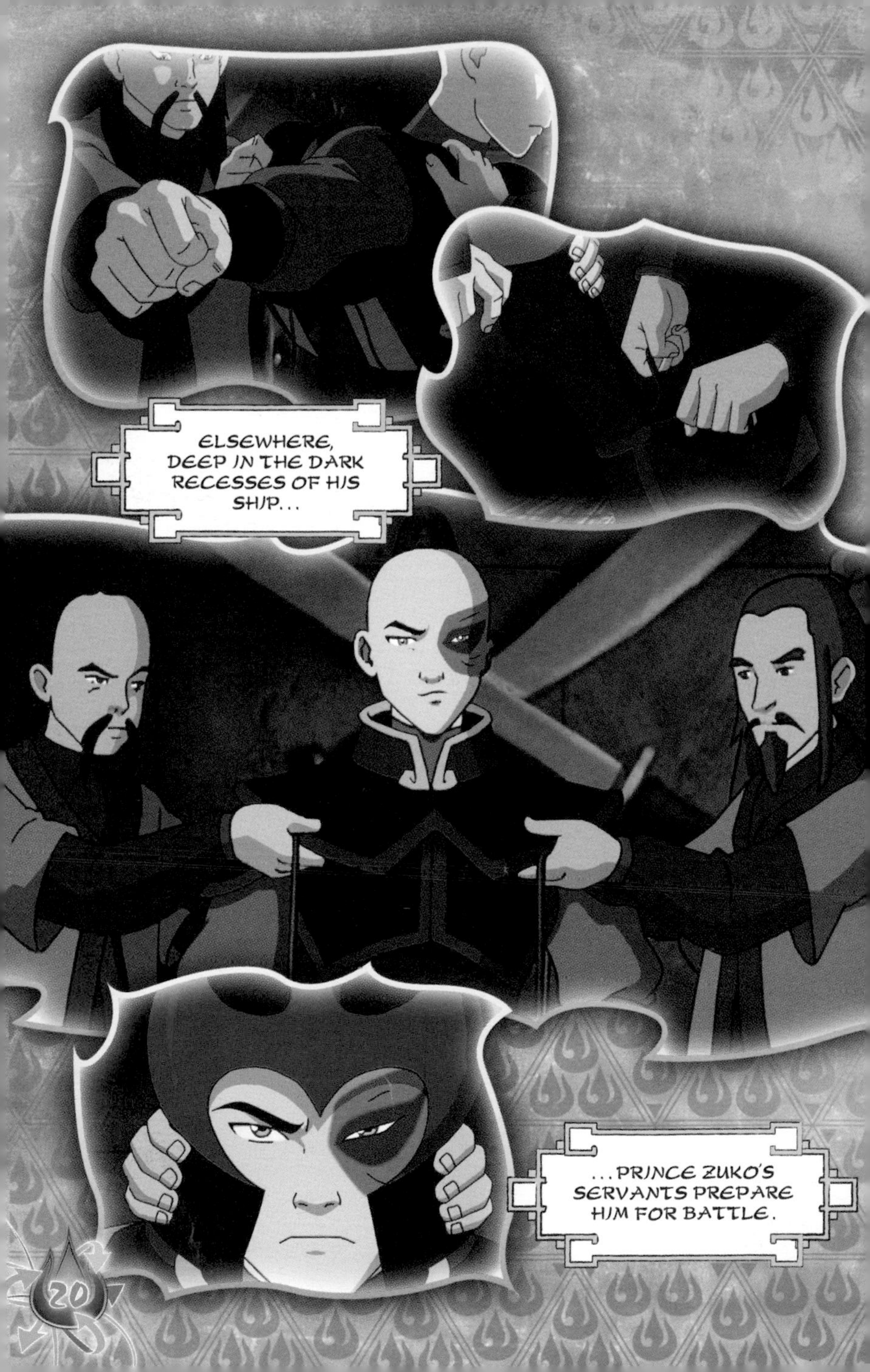
ELSEWHERE, DEEP IN THE DARK RECESSES OF HIS SHIP...
...PRINCE ZUKO'S SERVANTS PREPARE HIM FOR BATTLE.

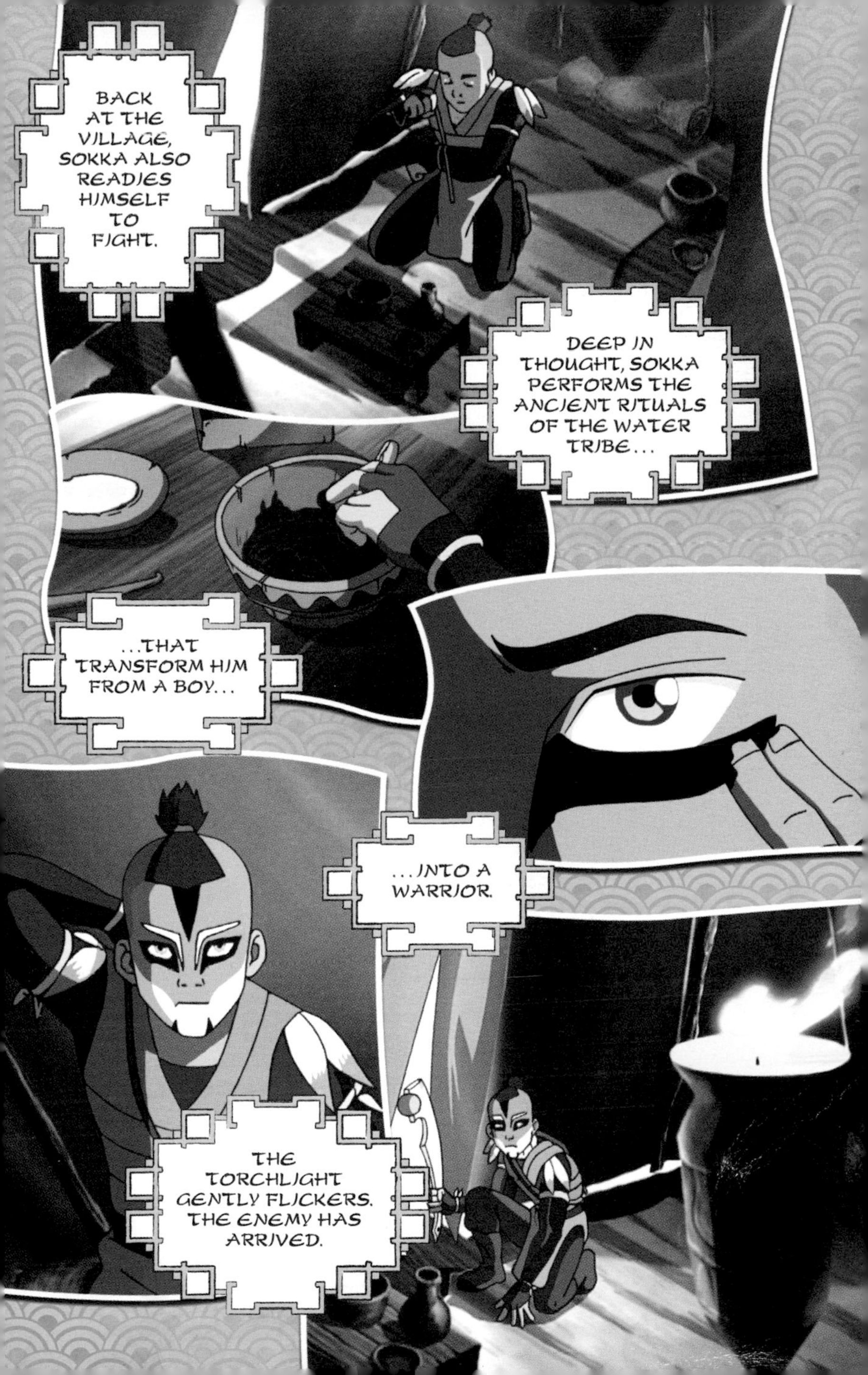
BACK AT THE VILLAGE, SOKKA ALSO READIES HIMSELF TO FIGHT.
DEEP IN THOUGHT, SOKKA PERFORMS THE ANCIENT RITUALS OF THE WATER TRIBE...
...THAT TRANSFORM HIM FROM A BOY...
...INTO A WARRIOR.
THE TORCHLIGHT GENTLY FLICKERS. THE ENEMY HAS ARRIVED.

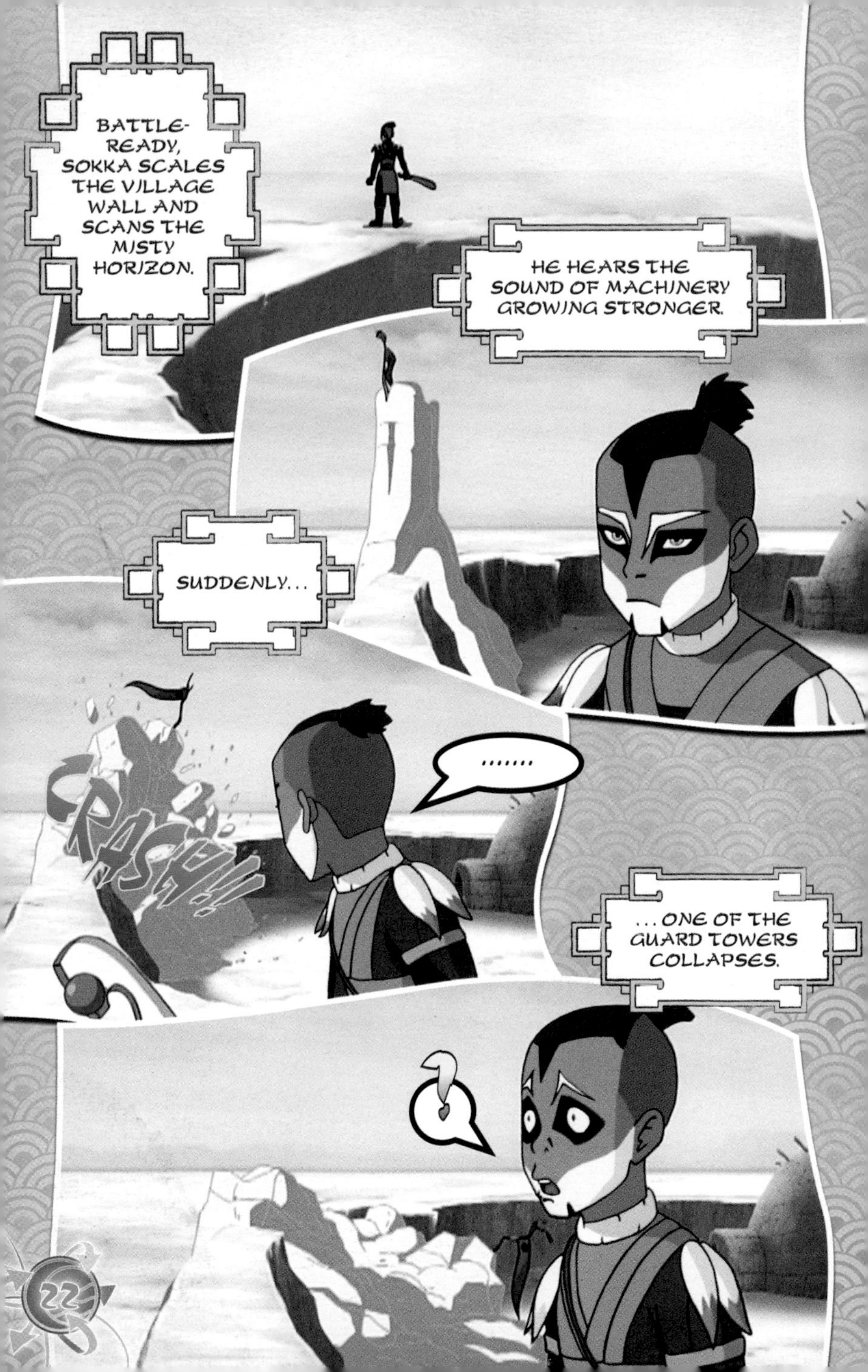

BATTLE-READY, SOKKA SCALES THE VILLAGE WALL AND SCANS THE MISTY HORIZON.
HE HEARS THE SOUND OF MACHINERY GROWING STRONGER.
SUDDENLY...
CRASH!!
......
...ONE OF THE GUARD TOWERS COLLAPSES.
?

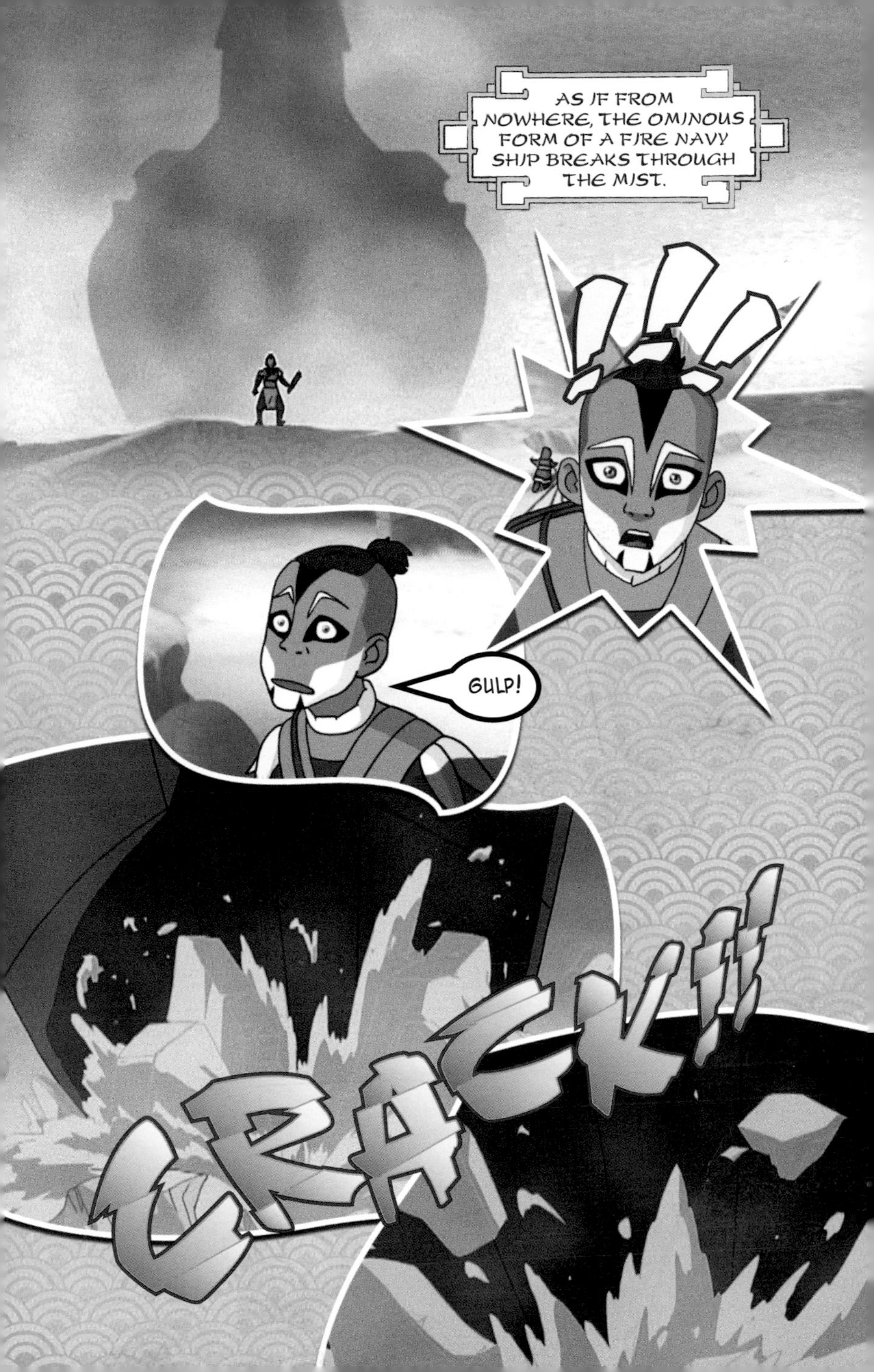
AS IF FROM NOWHERE, THE OMINOUS FORM OF A FIRE NAVY SHIP BREAKS THROUGH THE MIST.
GULP!
CRACK!!!

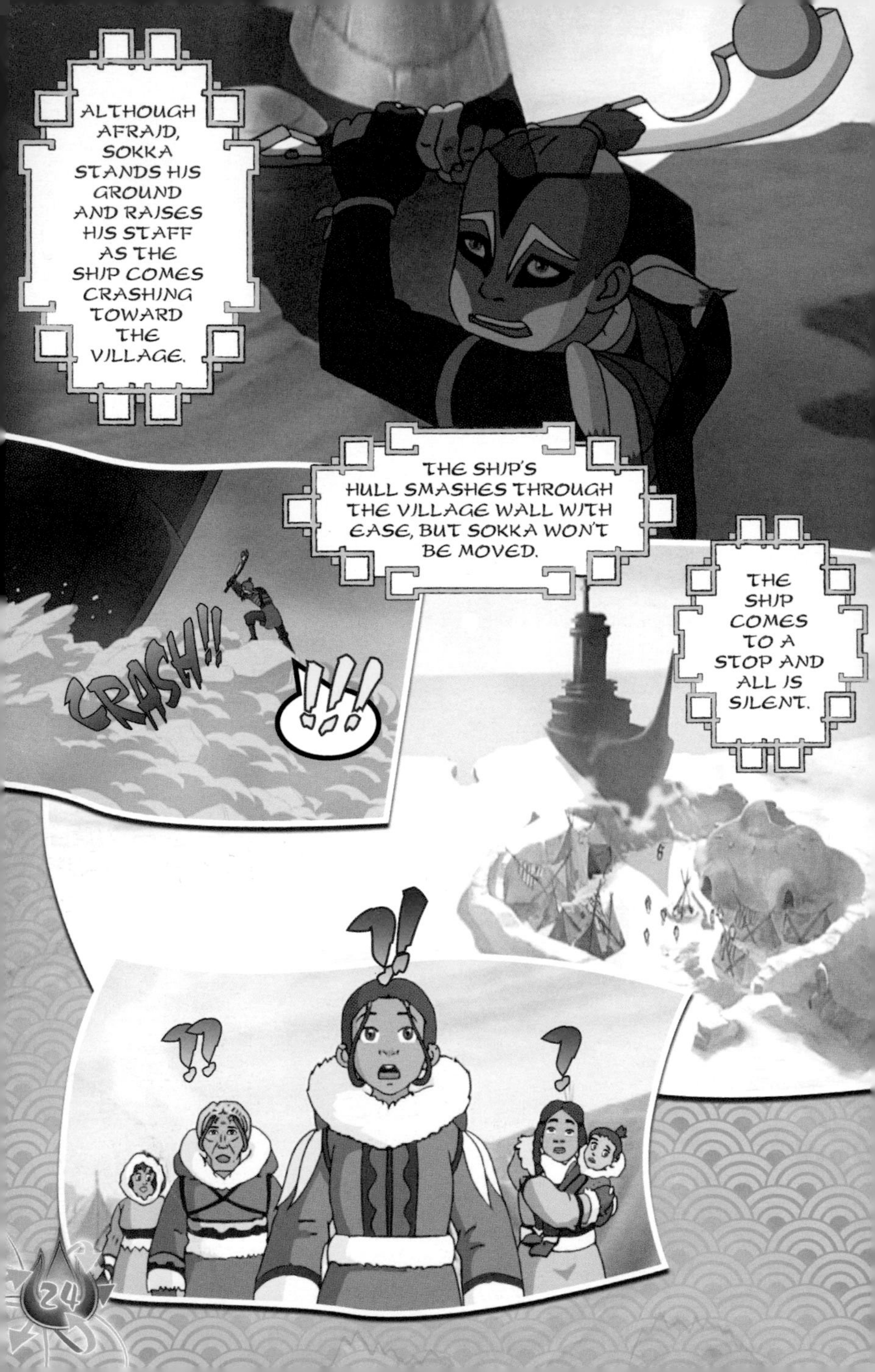
ALTHOUGH AFRAID, SOKKA STANDS HIS GROUND AND RAISES HIS STAFF AS THE SHIP COMES CRASHING TOWARD THE VILLAGE.
THE SHIP'S HULL SMASHES THROUGH THE VILLAGE WALL WITH EASE, BUT SOKKA WON'T BE MOVED.
CRASH!!
!!!
THE SHIP COMES TO A STOP AND ALL IS SILENT.
?!
??
?

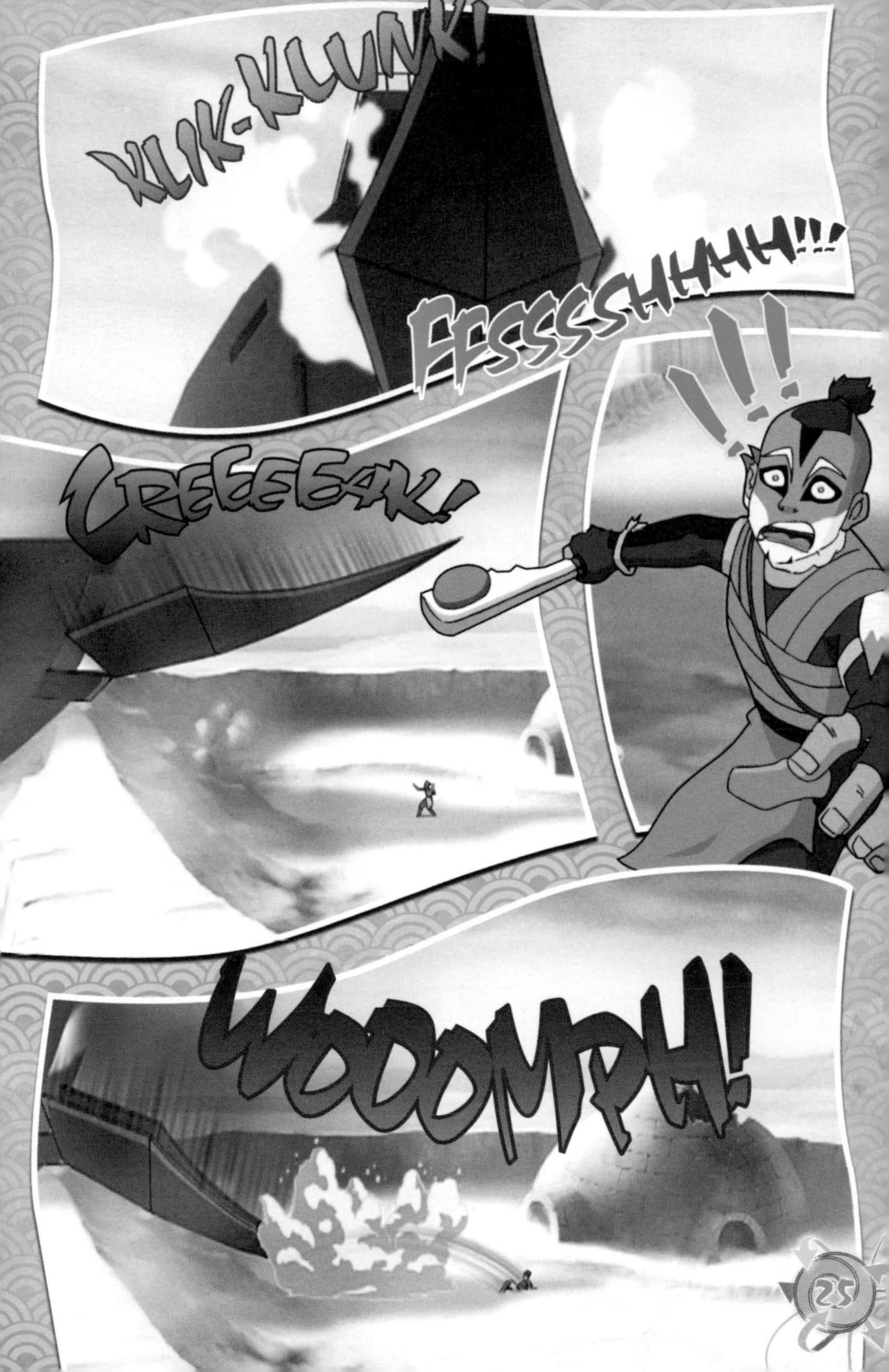
KLIK-KLUNK!
FFSSSSHHHH!!!
CREEEEAK!
!!!
WOOOMPH!

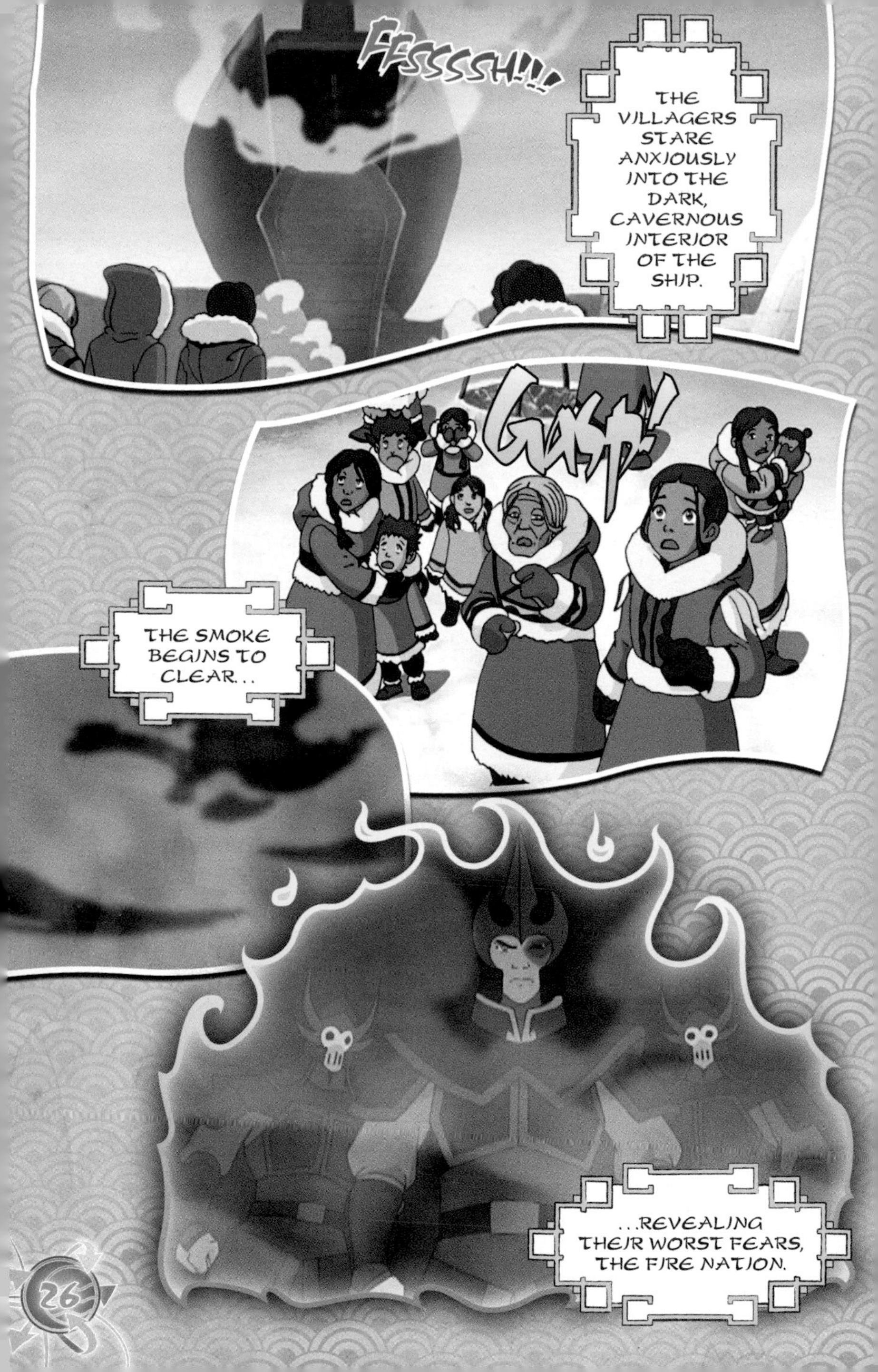
FFSSSSH!!!
THE VILLAGERS STARE ANXIOUSLY INTO THE DARK, CAVERNOUS INTERIOR OF THE SHIP.
GASP!
THE SMOKE BEGINS TO CLEAR...
...REVEALING THEIR WORST FEARS, THE FIRE NATION.

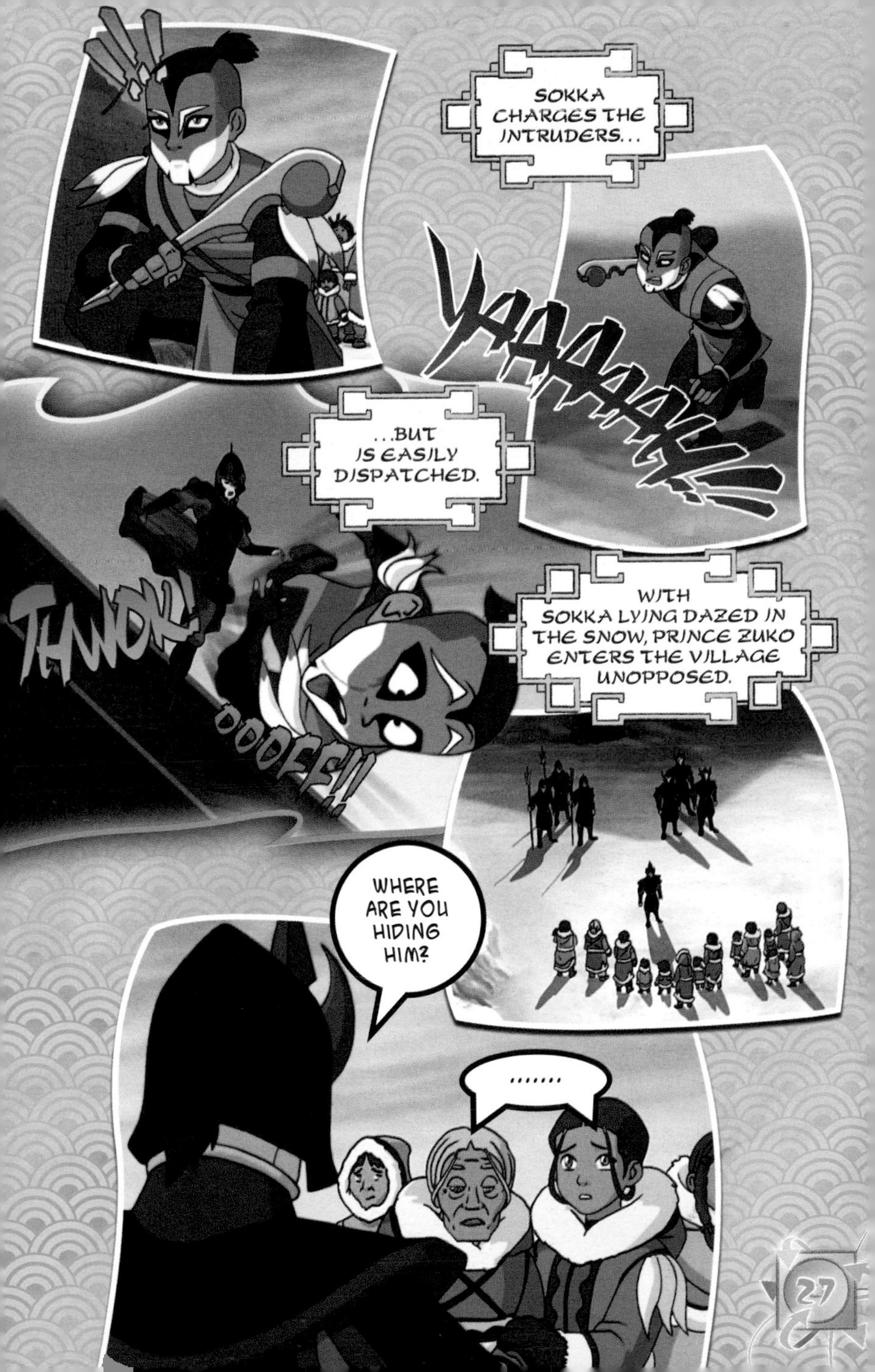
SOKKA CHARGES THE INTRUDERS...
YAAAAAAH!!!
...BUT IS EASILY DISPATCHED.
THWOK!
OOOFF!!
WITH SOKKA LYING DAZED IN THE SNOW, PRINCE ZUKO ENTERS THE VILLAGE UNOPPOSED.
WHERE ARE YOU HIDING HIM?
....

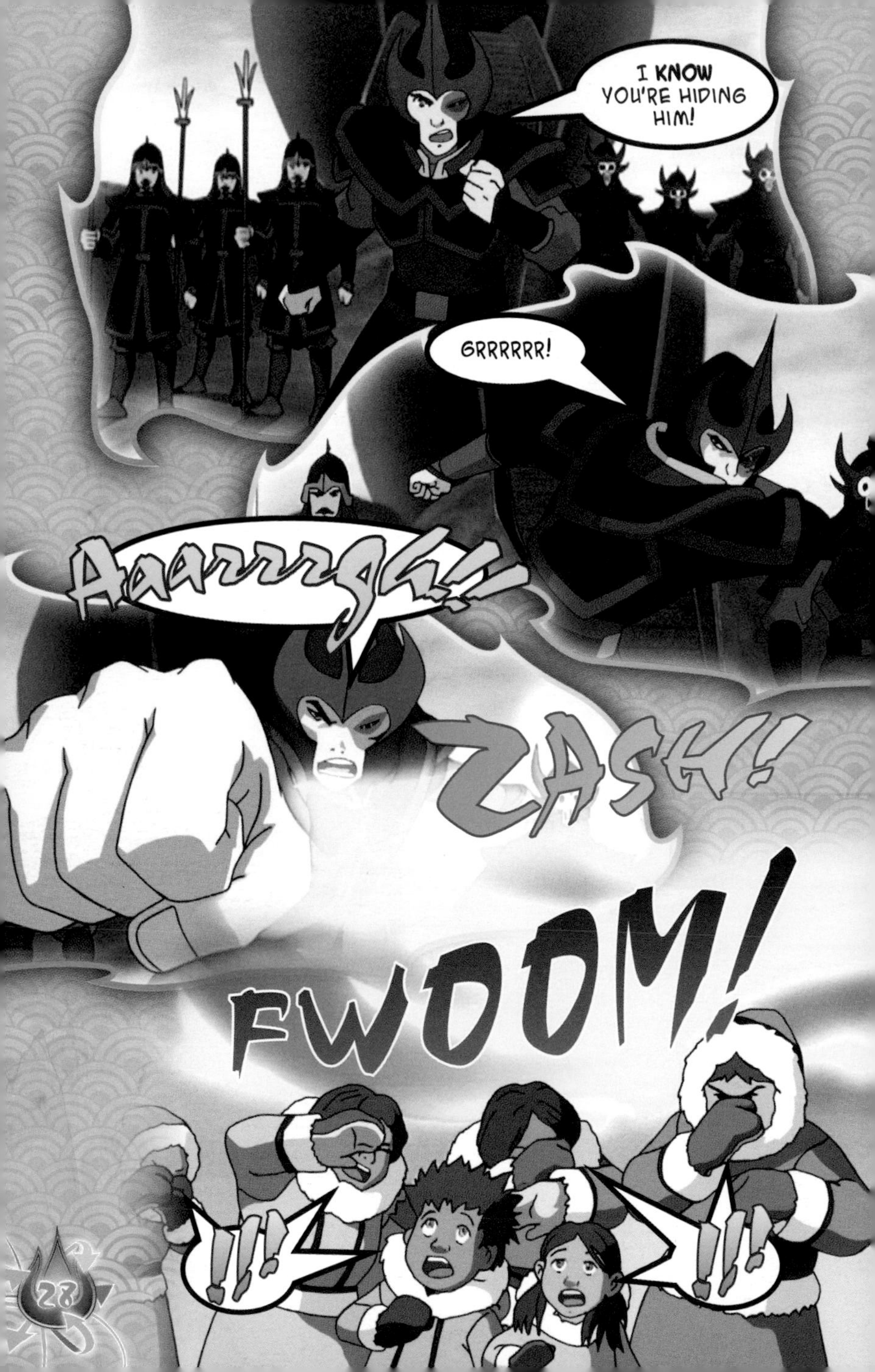
I KNOW YOU'RE HIDING HIM!
GRRRRRR!
Aaarrrgh!!
ZASH!
FWOOM!
!!
!!

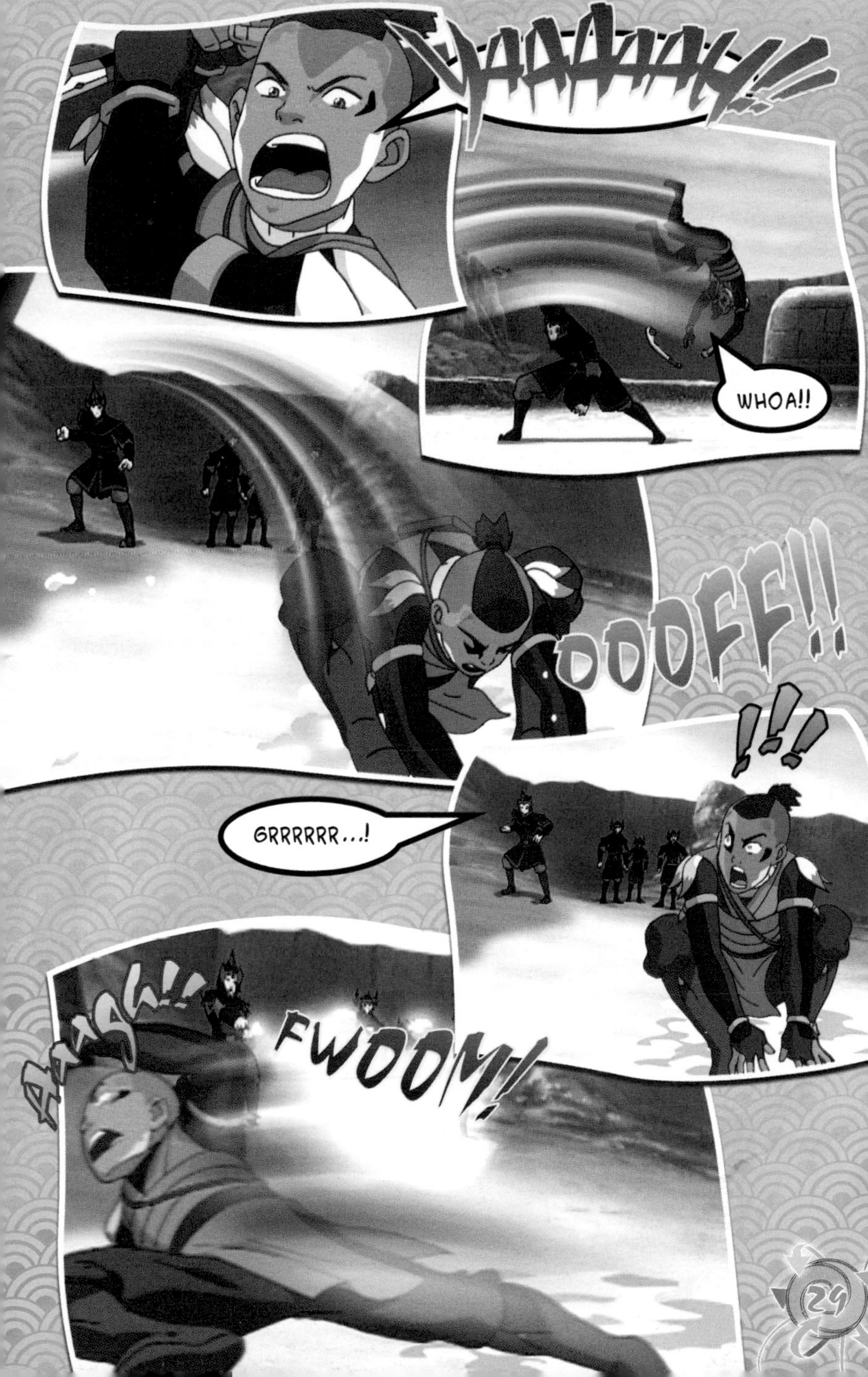
YAAAAAH!!
WHOA!!
OOOFF!!
GRRRRRR...!
!!!
AAAGH!!
FWOOM!

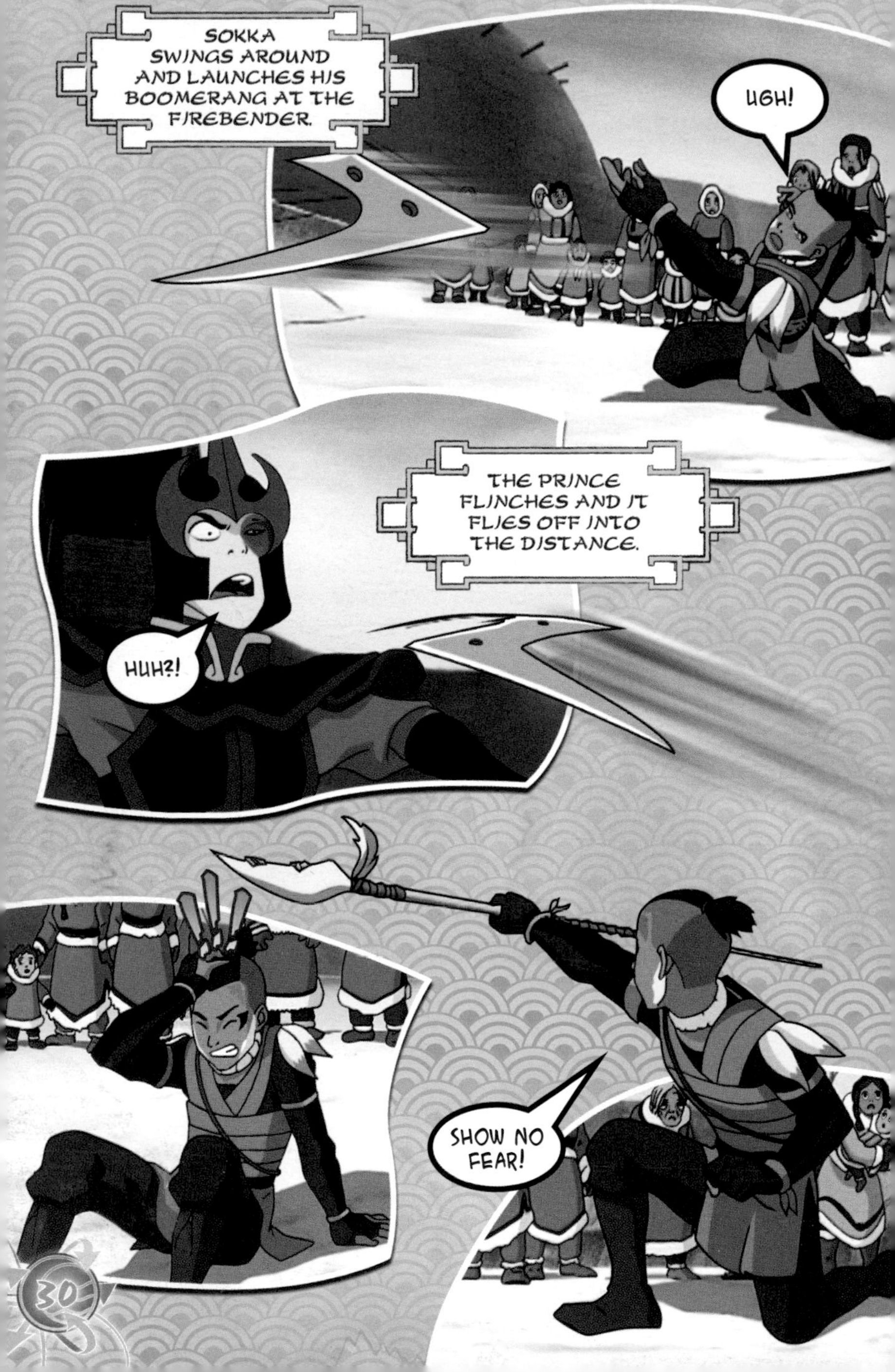
SOKKA SWINGS AROUND AND LAUNCHES HIS BOOMERANG AT THE FIREBENDER.
UGH!
THE PRINCE FLINCHES AND IT FLIES OFF INTO THE DISTANCE.
HUH?!
SHOW NO FEAR!

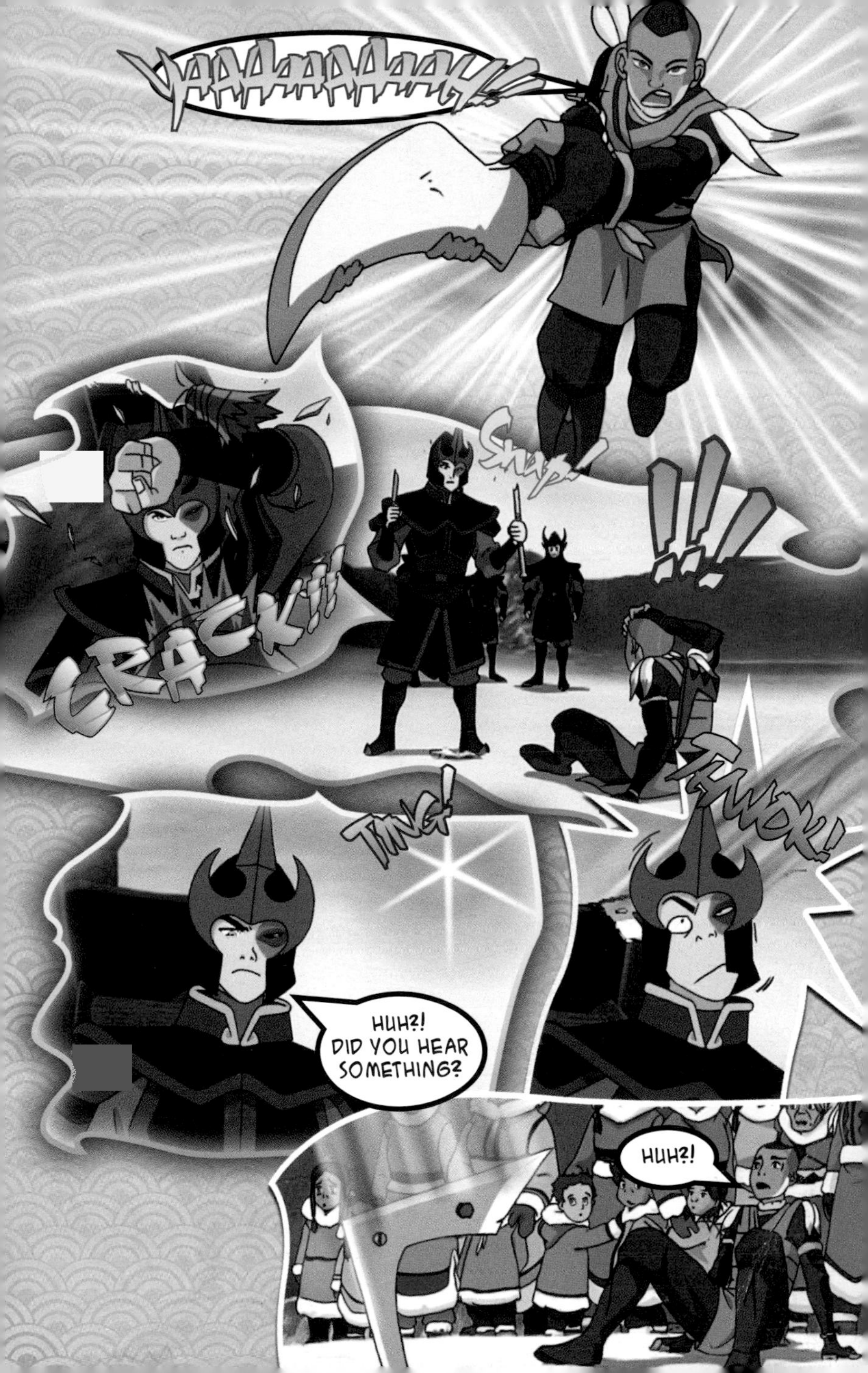
YAAAAAAAAAAH!!
CRACK!!!
Snap!
!!!
TING!
THWOK!
HUH?!
DID YOU HEAR
SOMETHING?
HUH?!

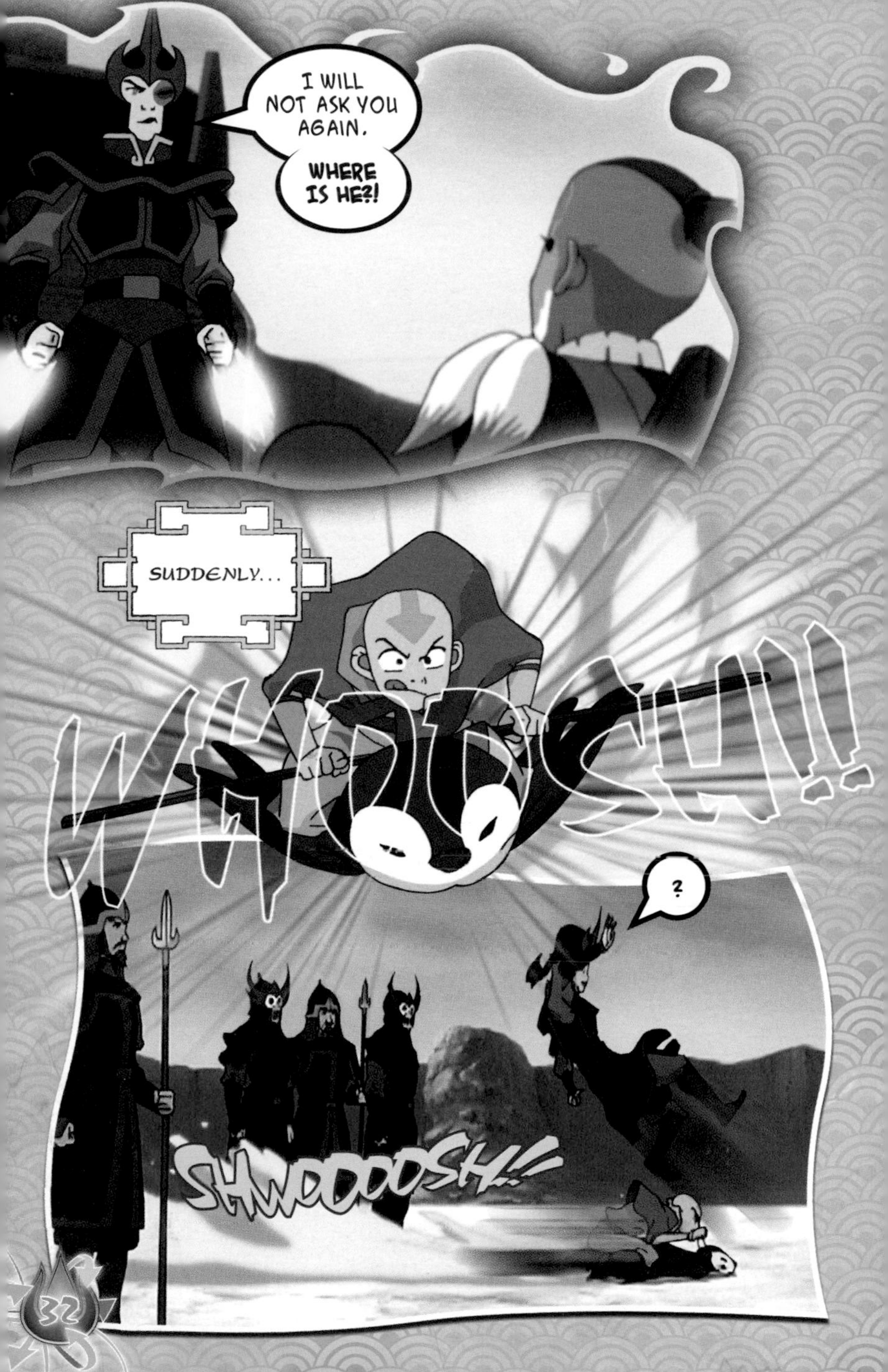
I WILL NOT ASK YOU AGAIN.
WHERE IS HE?!
SUDDENLY...
WHOOSH!!
?
SHWOOOOSH..!!

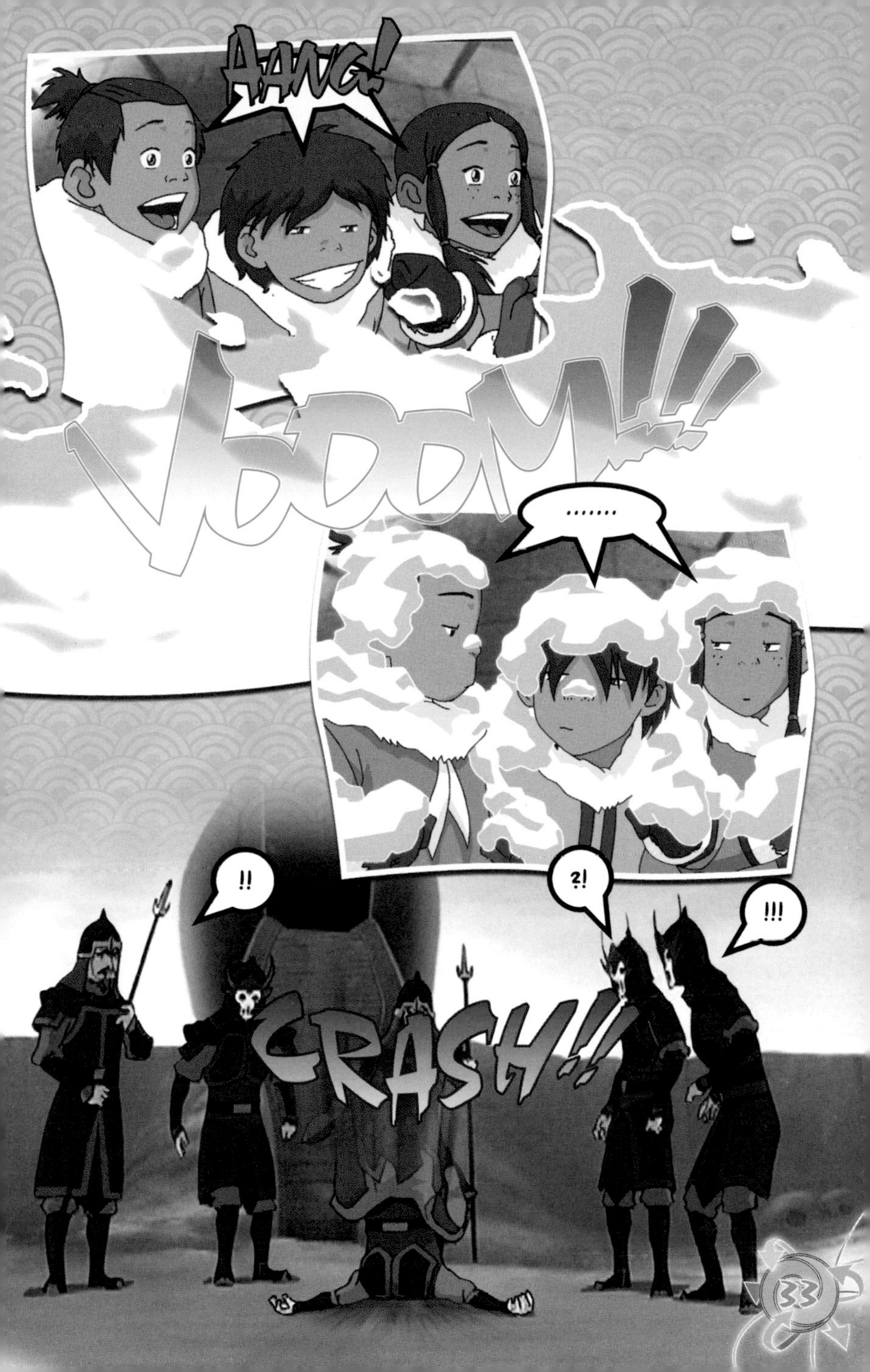

AANG!
VOOM!!!
....
!!
?!
!!!
CRASH!!

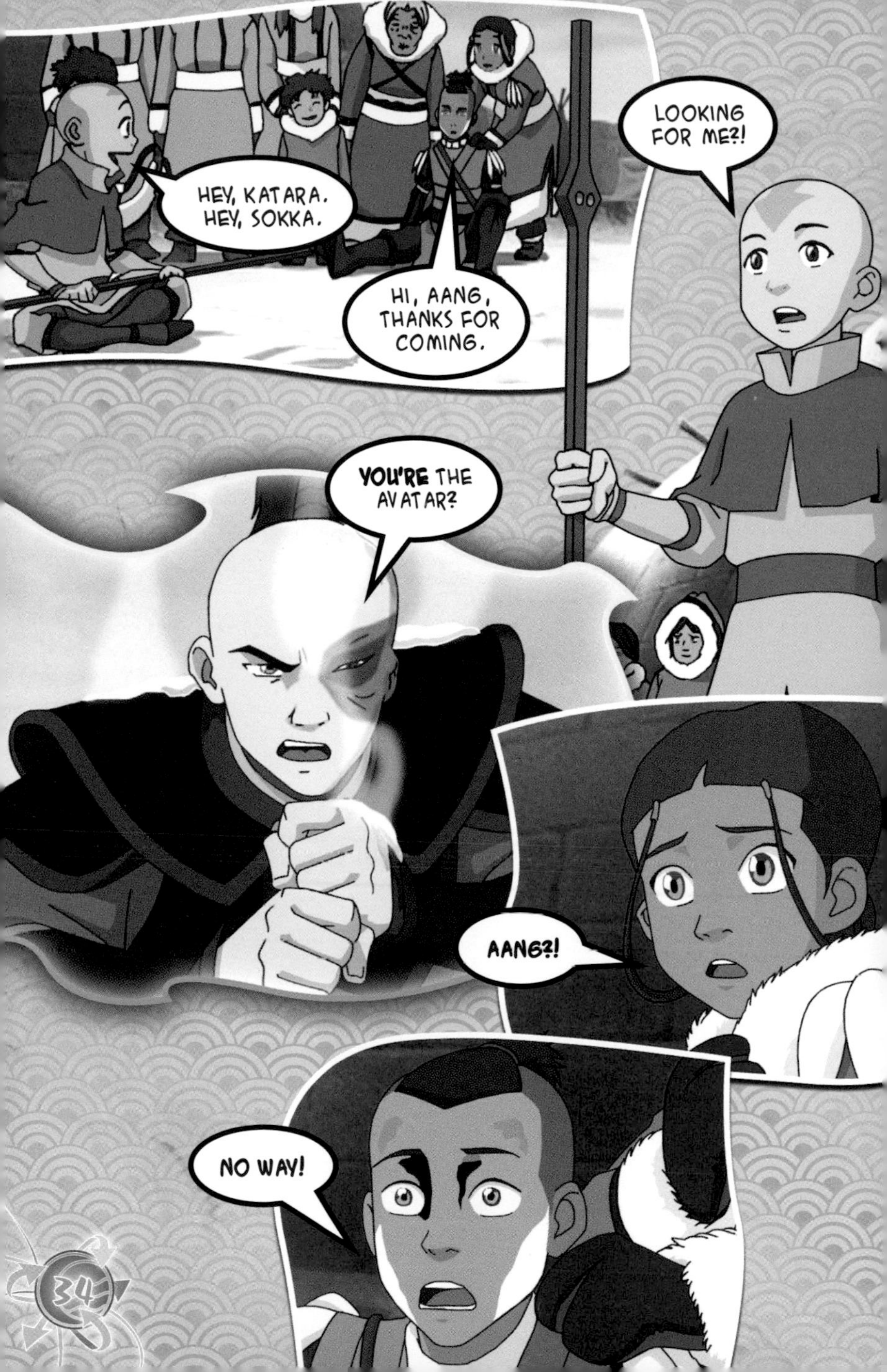
HEY, KATARA.
HEY, SOKKA.
HI, AANG, THANKS FOR COMING.
LOOKING FOR ME?!
YOU'RE THE AVATAR?
AANG?!
NO WAY!

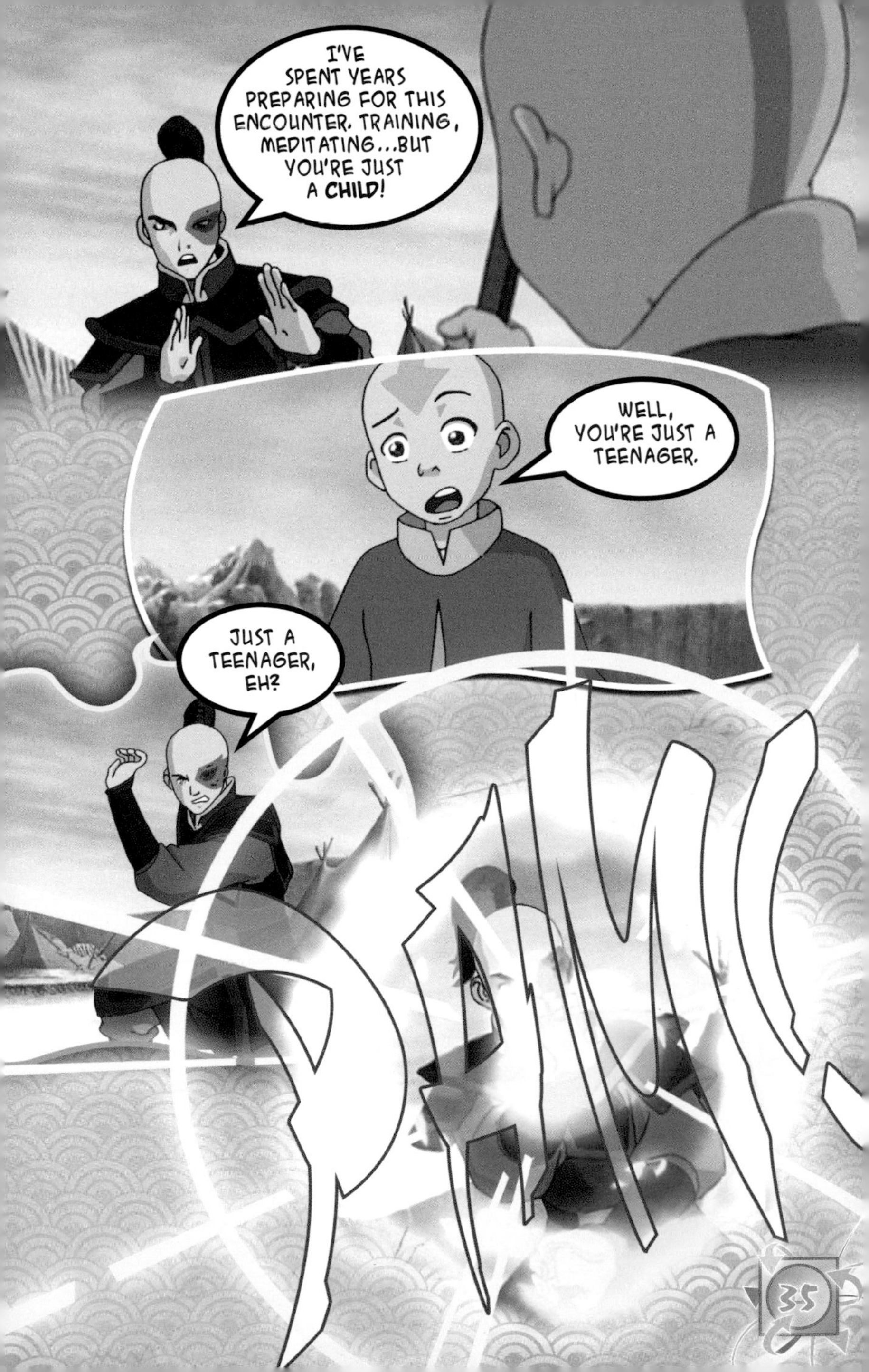
I'VE SPENT YEARS PREPARING FOR THIS ENCOUNTER. TRAINING, MEDITATING...BUT YOU'RE JUST A **CHILD**!
WELL, YOU'RE JUST A TEENAGER.
JUST A TEENAGER, EH?
BAM!

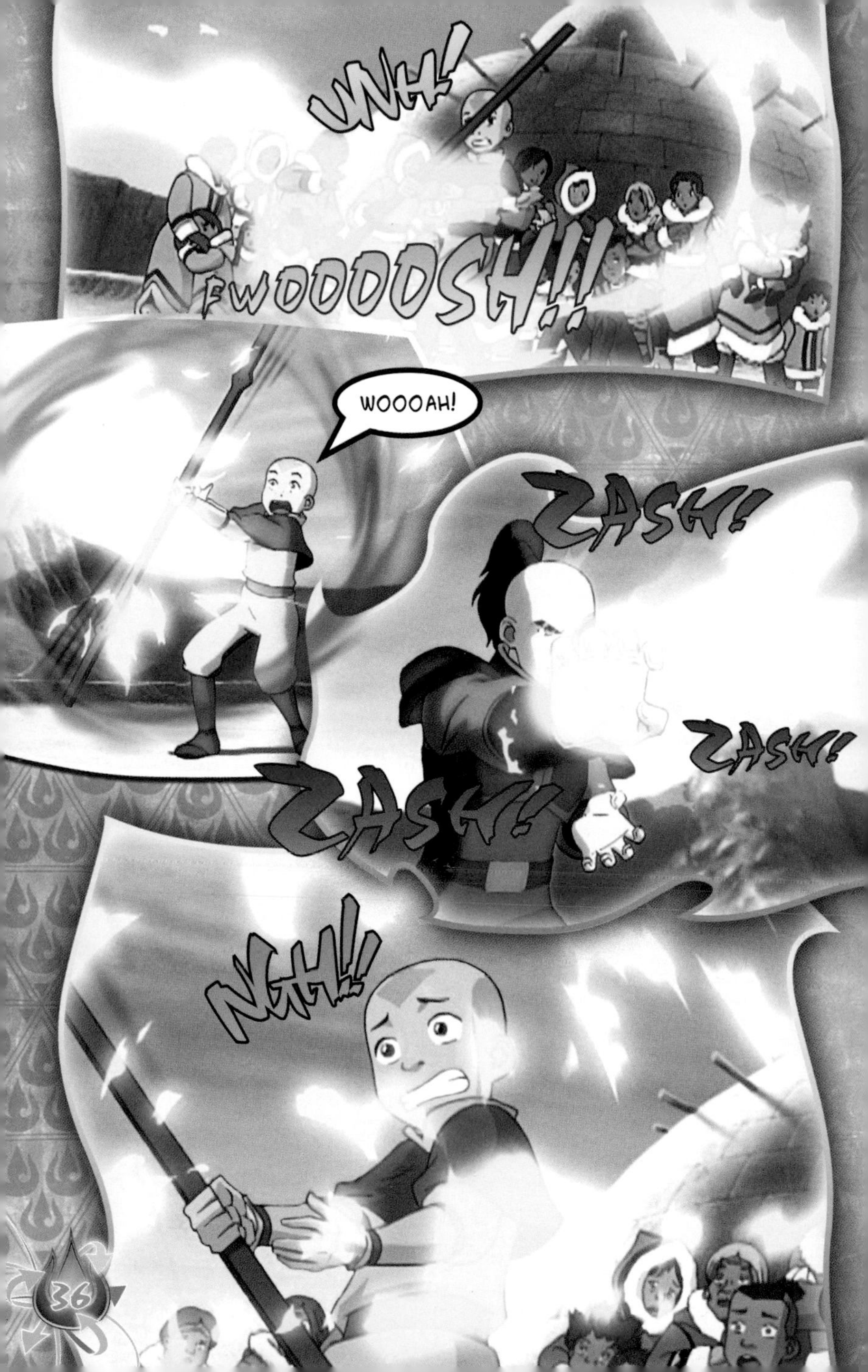
UNH!
FWOOOOSH!!
WOOOAH!
ZASH!
ZASH!
ZASH!
NGH!!

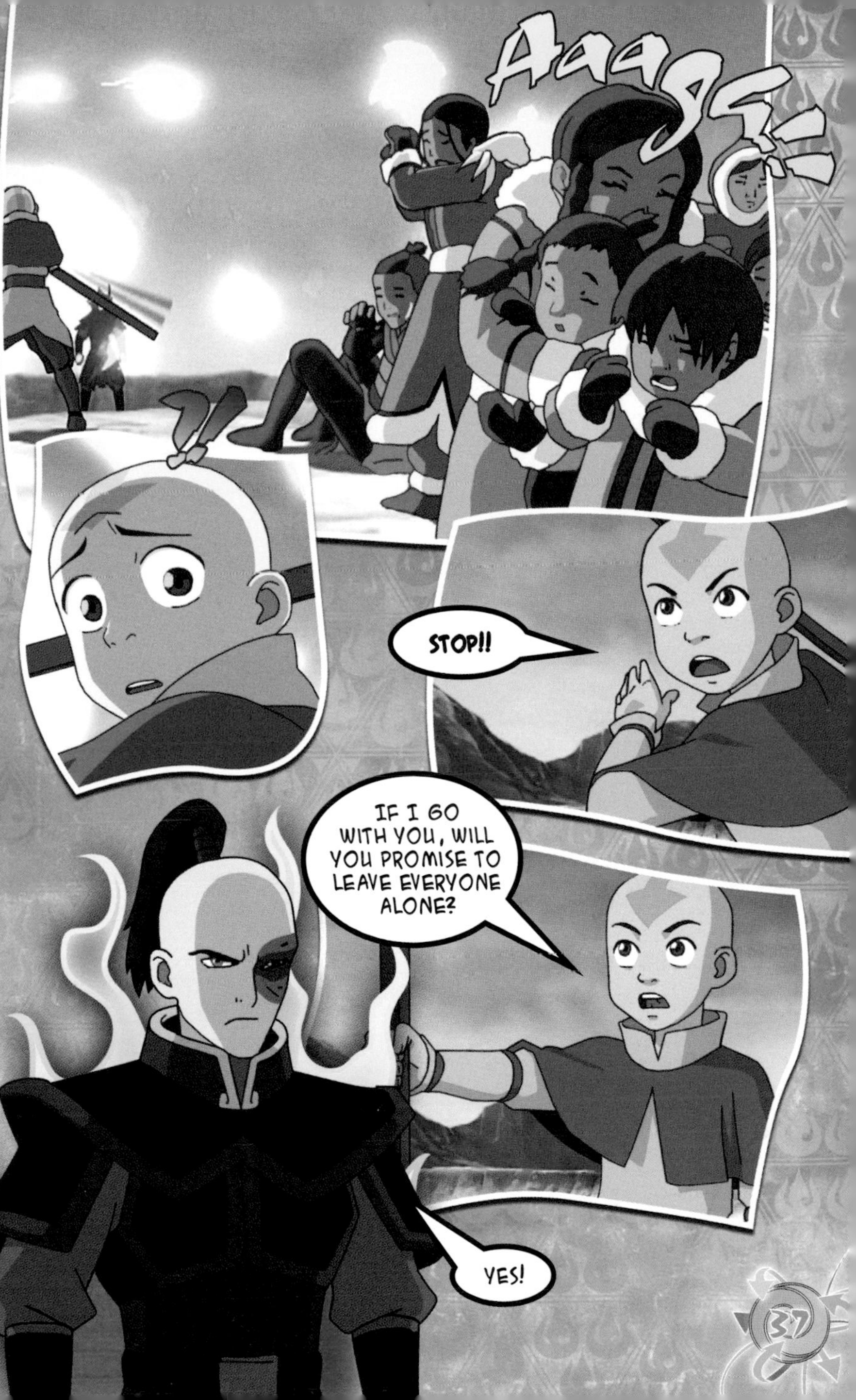

Aaagh!!
STOP!!
IF I GO WITH YOU, WILL YOU PROMISE TO LEAVE EVERYONE ALONE?
YES!

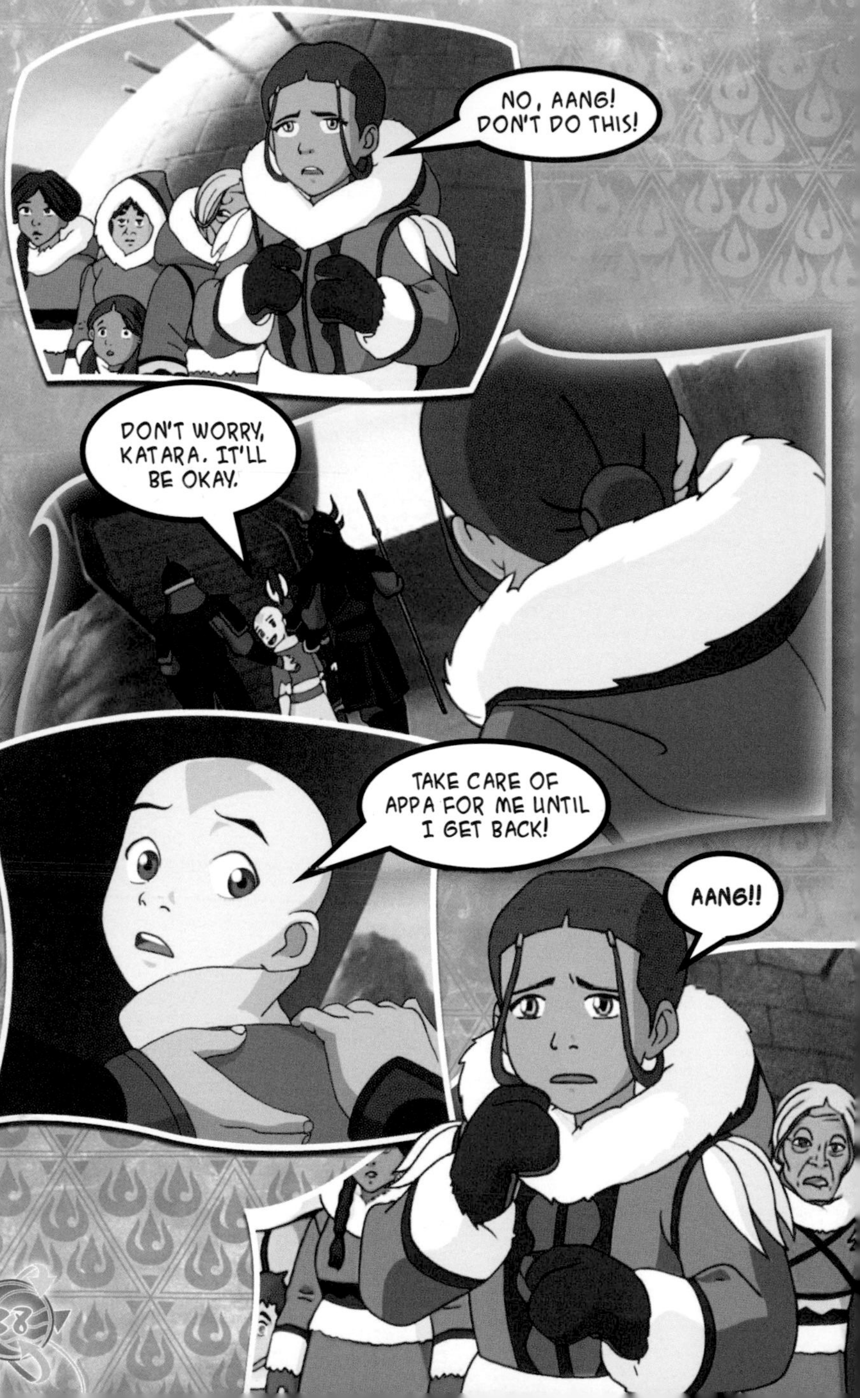
NO, AANG! DON'T DO THIS!
DON'T WORRY, KATARA. IT'LL BE OKAY.
TAKE CARE OF APPA FOR ME UNTIL I GET BACK!
AANG!!

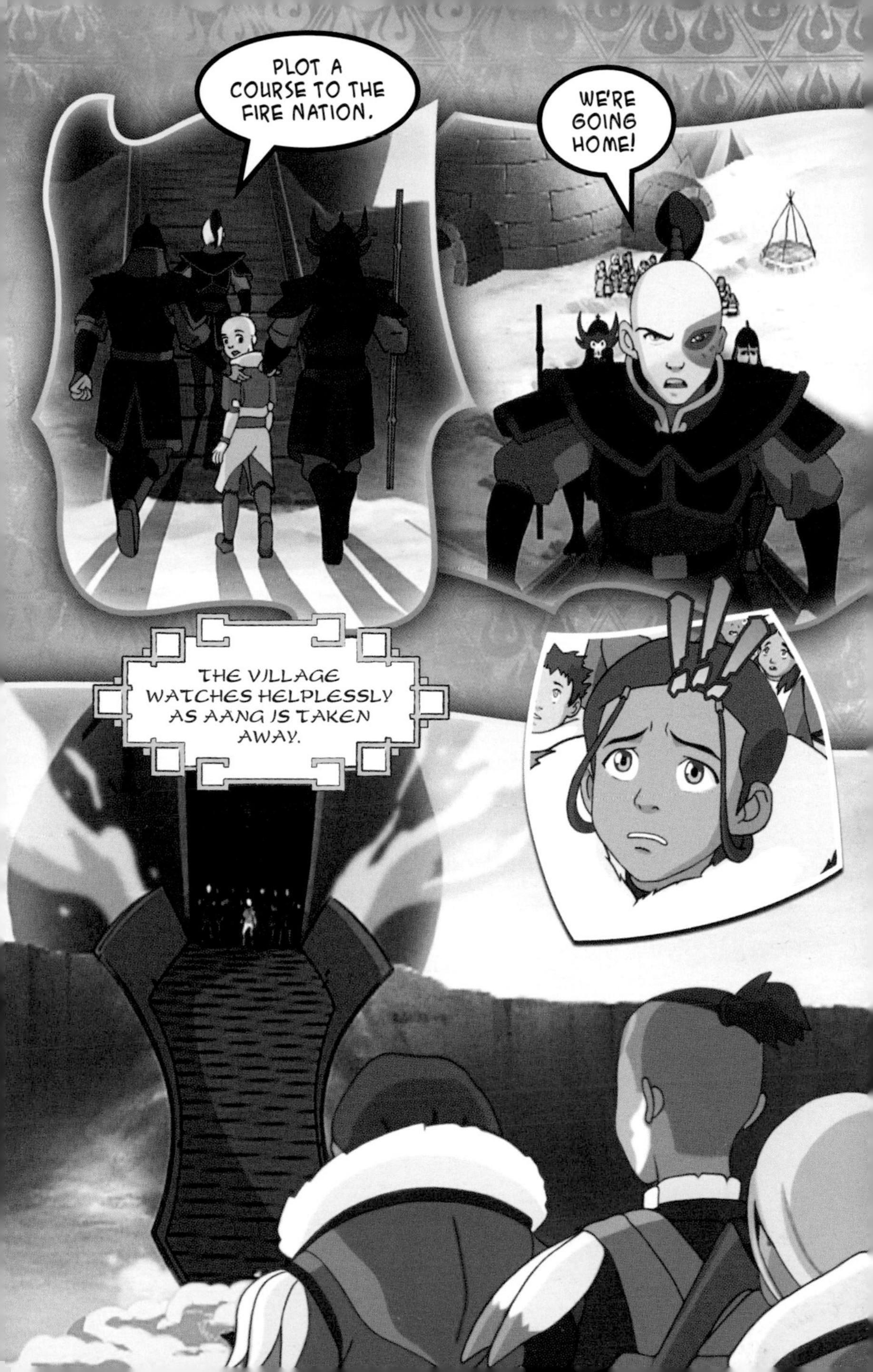
PLOT A COURSE TO THE FIRE NATION.
WE'RE GOING HOME!
THE VILLAGE WATCHES HELPLESSLY AS AANG IS TAKEN AWAY.

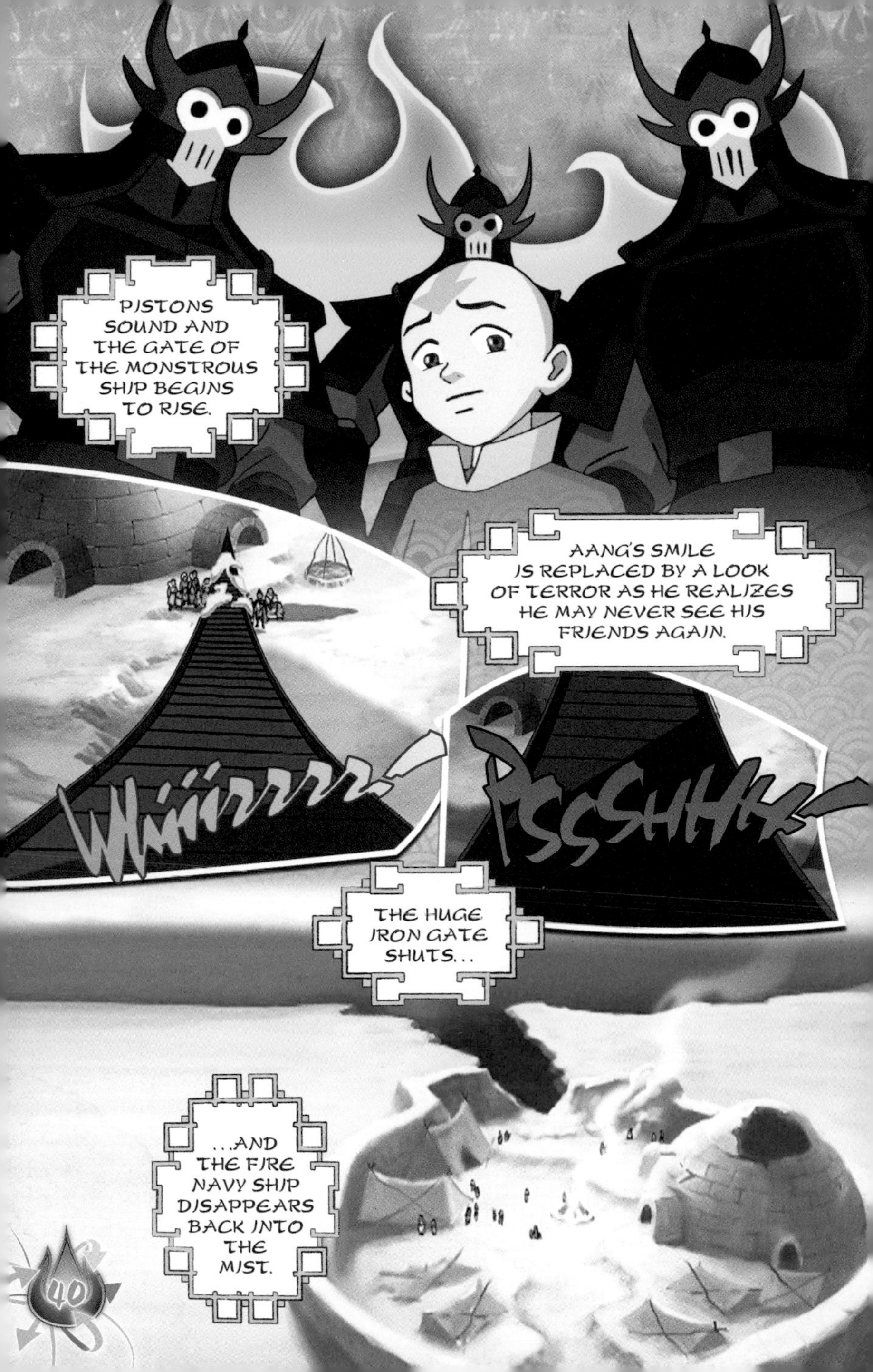
PISTONS SOUND AND THE GATE OF THE MONSTROUS SHIP BEGINS TO RISE.
AANG'S SMILE IS REPLACED BY A LOOK OF TERROR AS HE REALIZES HE MAY NEVER SEE HIS FRIENDS AGAIN.
WHIIIRRRRR!
PSSSHHHH!
THE HUGE IRON GATE SHUTS...
...AND THE FIRE NAVY SHIP DISAPPEARS BACK INTO THE MIST.
40

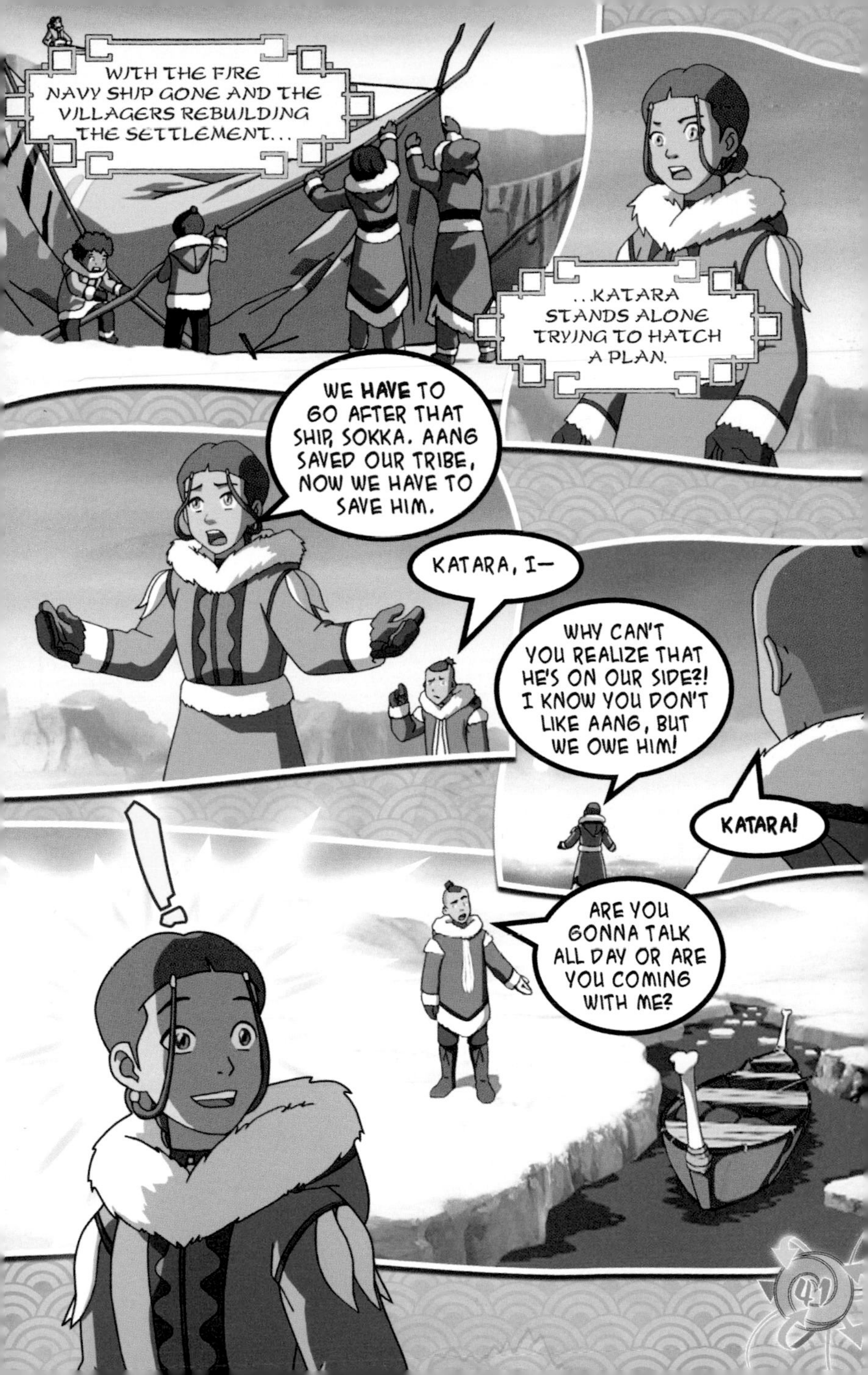
WITH THE FIRE NAVY SHIP GONE AND THE VILLAGERS REBUILDING THE SETTLEMENT...
...KATARA STANDS ALONE TRYING TO HATCH A PLAN.
WE **HAVE** TO GO AFTER THAT SHIP, SOKKA. AANG SAVED OUR TRIBE, NOW WE HAVE TO SAVE HIM.
KATARA, I—
WHY CAN'T YOU REALIZE THAT HE'S ON OUR SIDE?! I KNOW YOU DON'T LIKE AANG, BUT WE OWE HIM!
KATARA!
ARE YOU GONNA TALK ALL DAY OR ARE YOU COMING WITH ME?

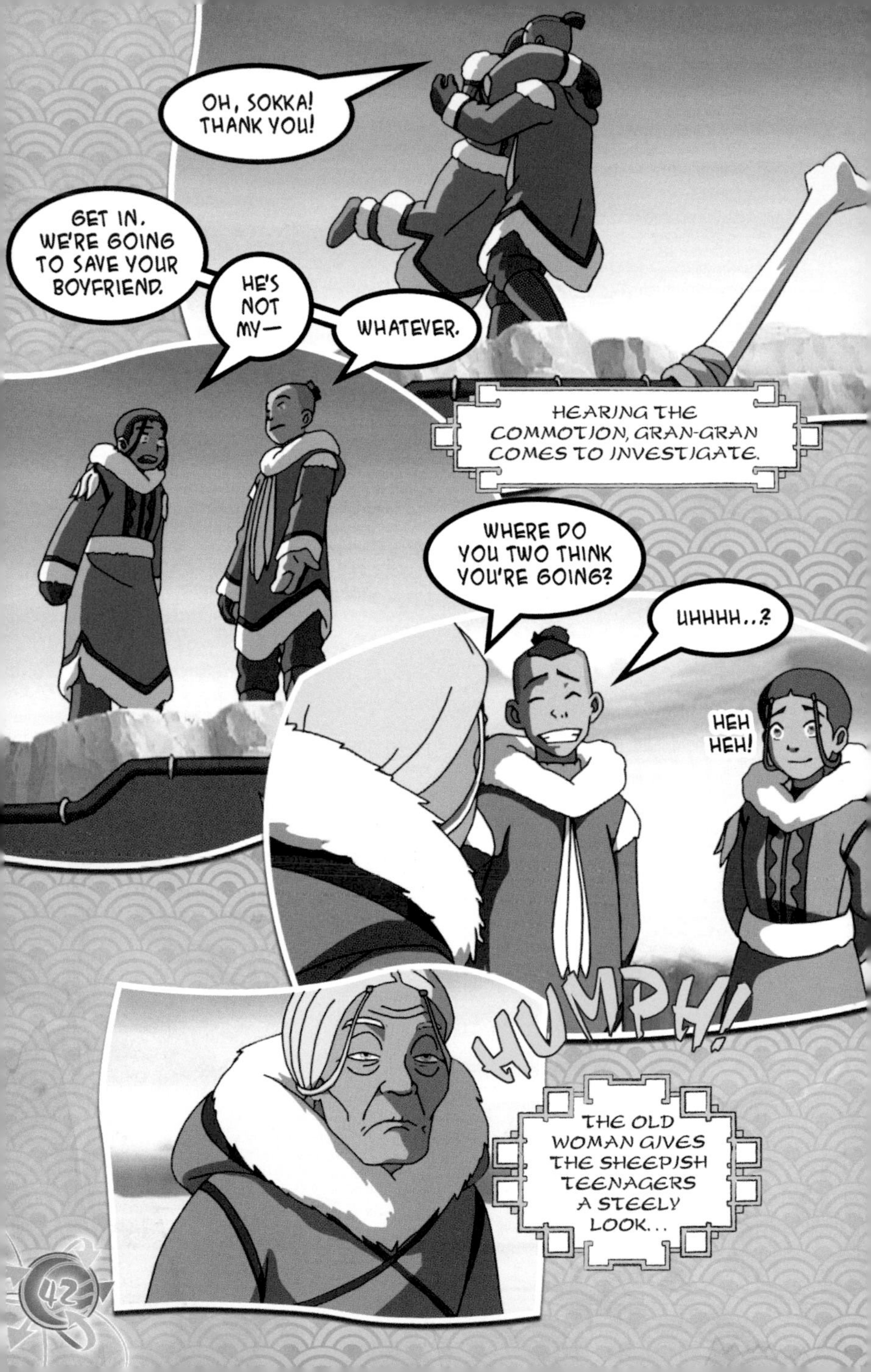
OH, SOKKA! THANK YOU!
GET IN. WE'RE GOING TO SAVE YOUR BOYFRIEND.
HE'S NOT MY—
WHATEVER.
HEARING THE COMMOTION, GRAN-GRAN COMES TO INVESTIGATE.
WHERE DO YOU TWO THINK YOU'RE GOING?
UHHHH...?
HEH HEH!
HUMPH!
THE OLD WOMAN GIVES THE SHEEPISH TEENAGERS A STEELY LOOK...

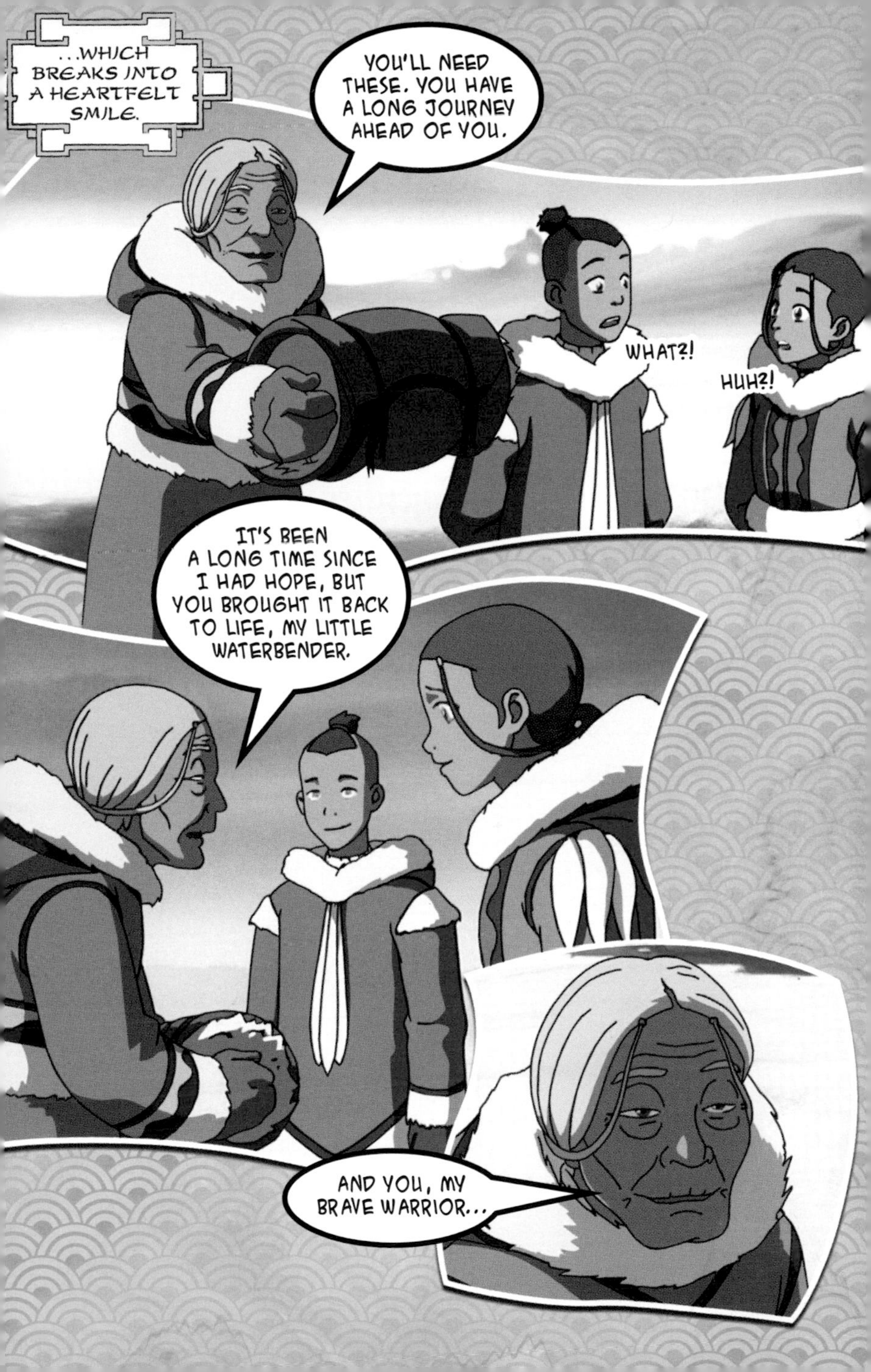
...WHICH BREAKS INTO A HEARTFELT SMILE.
YOU'LL NEED THESE. YOU HAVE A LONG JOURNEY AHEAD OF YOU.
WHAT?!
HUH?!
IT'S BEEN A LONG TIME SINCE I HAD HOPE, BUT YOU BROUGHT IT BACK TO LIFE, MY LITTLE WATERBENDER.
AND YOU, MY BRAVE WARRIOR...

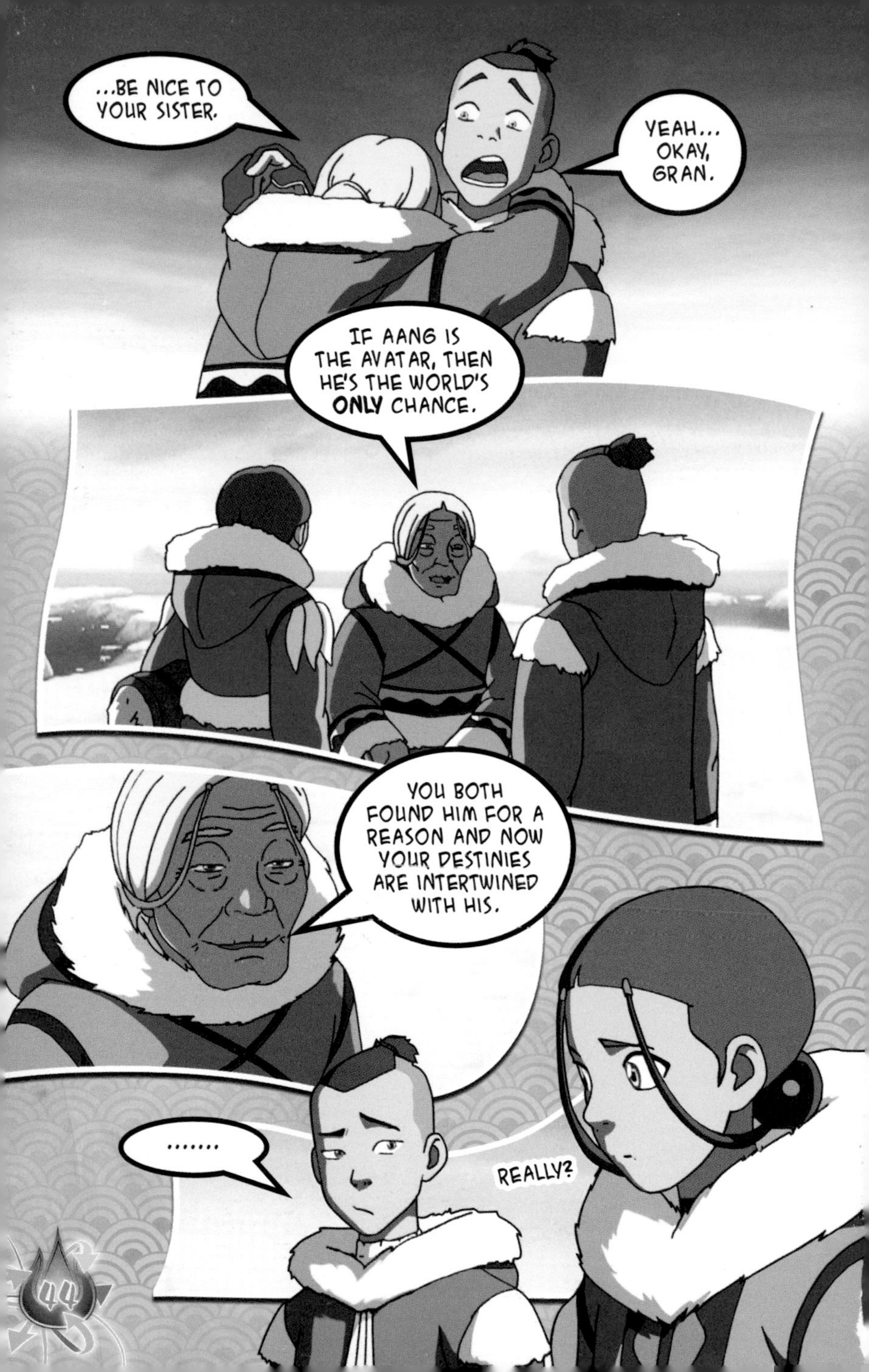
...BE NICE TO YOUR SISTER.
YEAH... OKAY, GRAN.
IF AANG IS THE AVATAR, THEN HE'S THE WORLD'S **ONLY** CHANCE.
YOU BOTH FOUND HIM FOR A REASON AND NOW YOUR DESTINIES ARE INTERTWINED WITH HIS.
....
REALLY?

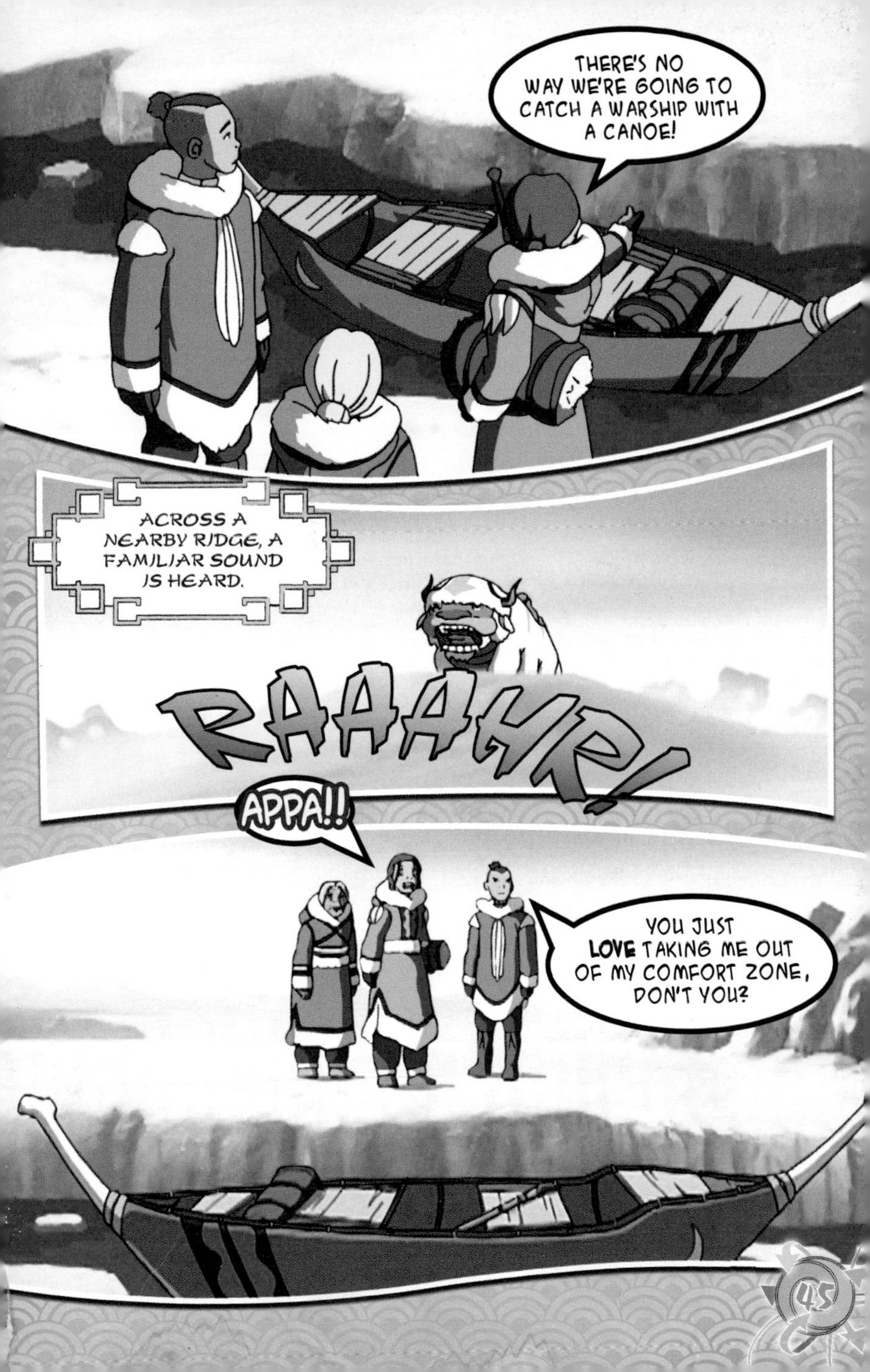
THERE'S NO WAY WE'RE GOING TO CATCH A WARSHIP WITH A CANOE!
ACROSS A NEARBY RIDGE, A FAMILIAR SOUND IS HEARD.
RAAAHR!
APPA!!
YOU JUST **LOVE** TAKING ME OUT OF MY COMFORT ZONE, DON'T YOU?

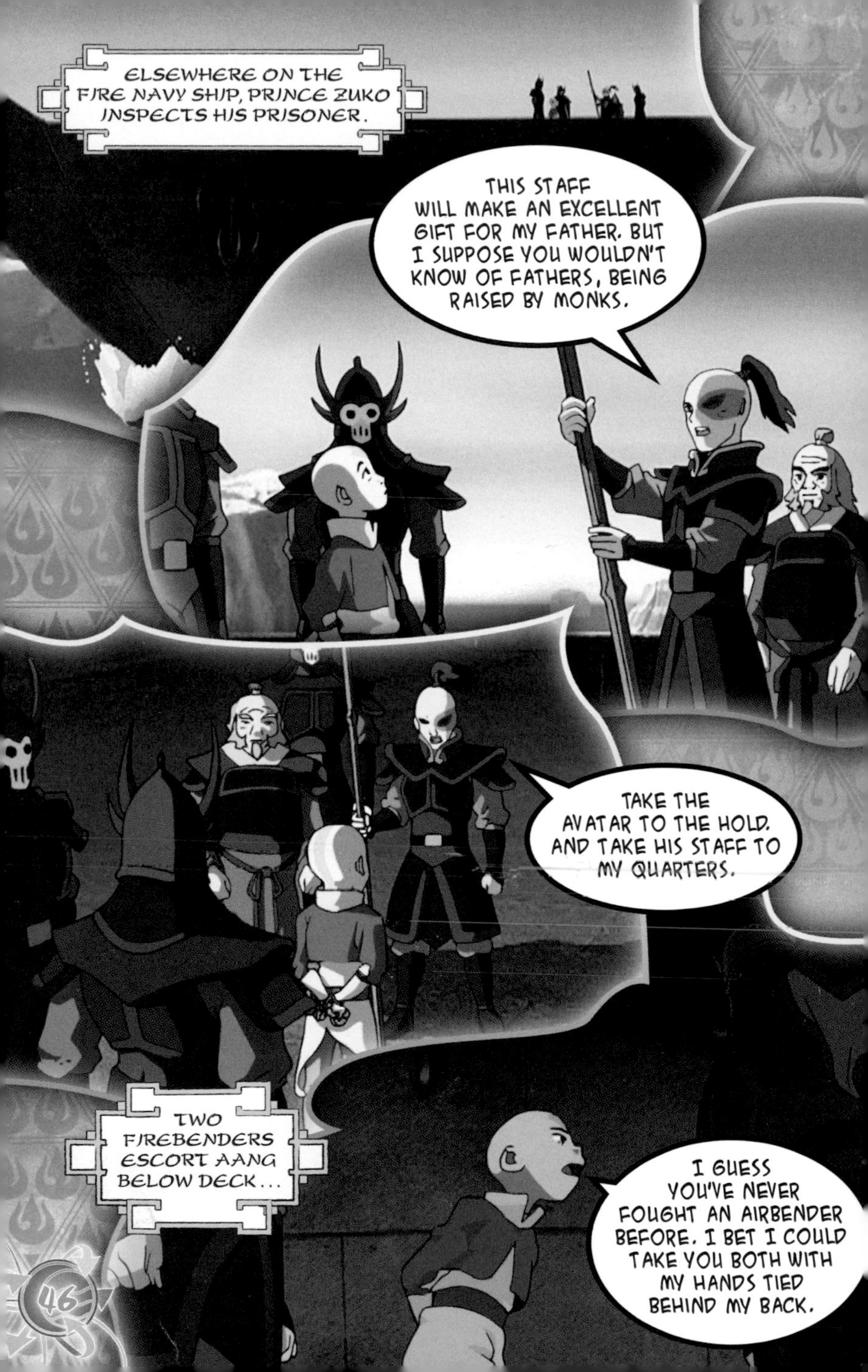
ELSEWHERE ON THE FIRE NAVY SHIP, PRINCE ZUKO INSPECTS HIS PRISONER.
THIS STAFF WILL MAKE AN EXCELLENT GIFT FOR MY FATHER. BUT I SUPPOSE YOU WOULDN'T KNOW OF FATHERS, BEING RAISED BY MONKS.
TAKE THE AVATAR TO THE HOLD. AND TAKE HIS STAFF TO MY QUARTERS.
TWO FIREBENDERS ESCORT AANG BELOW DECK...
I GUESS YOU'VE NEVER FOUGHT AN AIRBENDER BEFORE. I BET I COULD TAKE YOU BOTH WITH MY HANDS TIED BEHIND MY BACK.

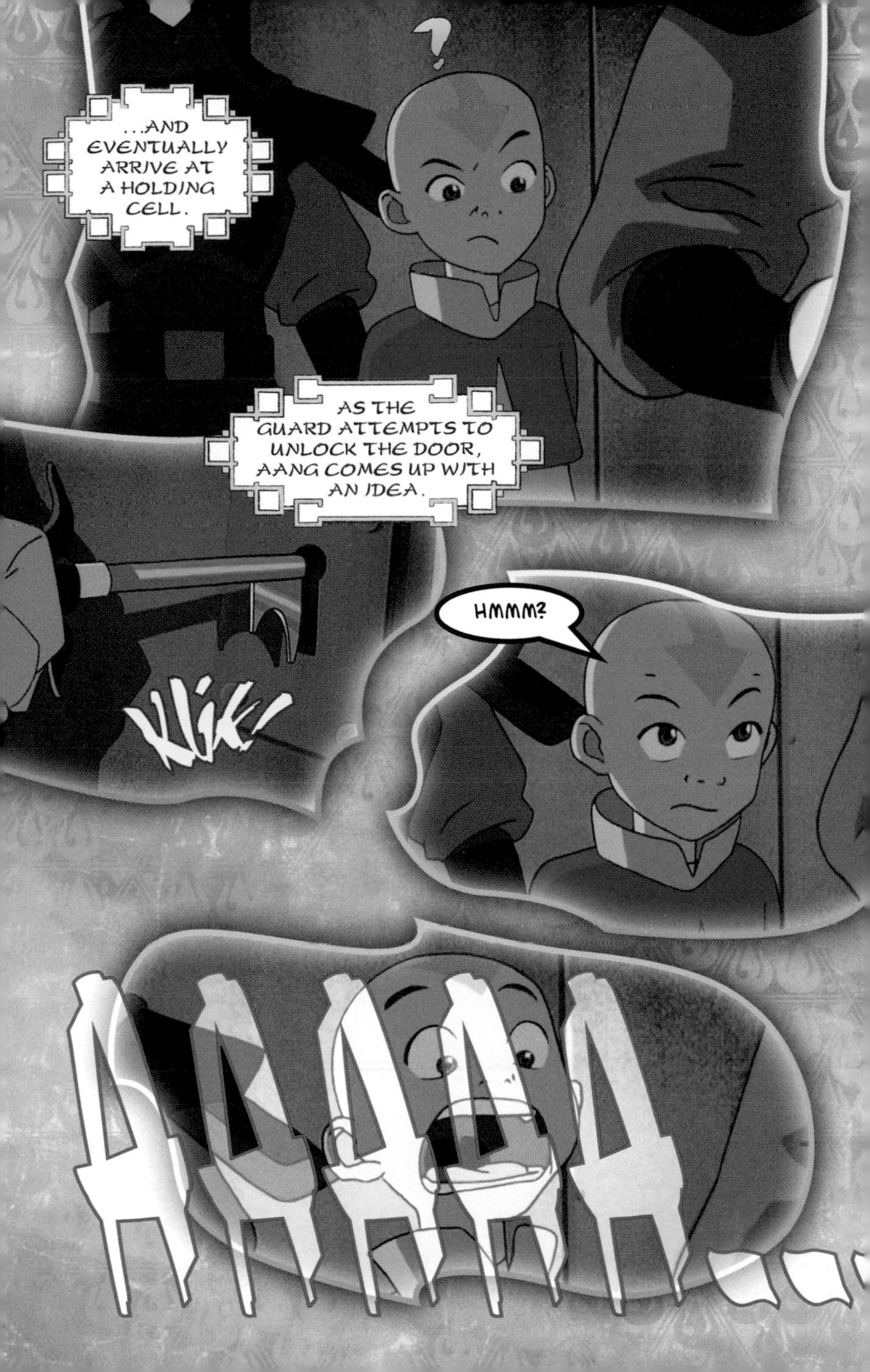
?
...AND EVENTUALLY ARRIVE AT A HOLDING CELL.
AS THE GUARD ATTEMPTS TO UNLOCK THE DOOR, AANG COMES UP WITH AN IDEA.
KLIK!
HMMM?
AAAA...

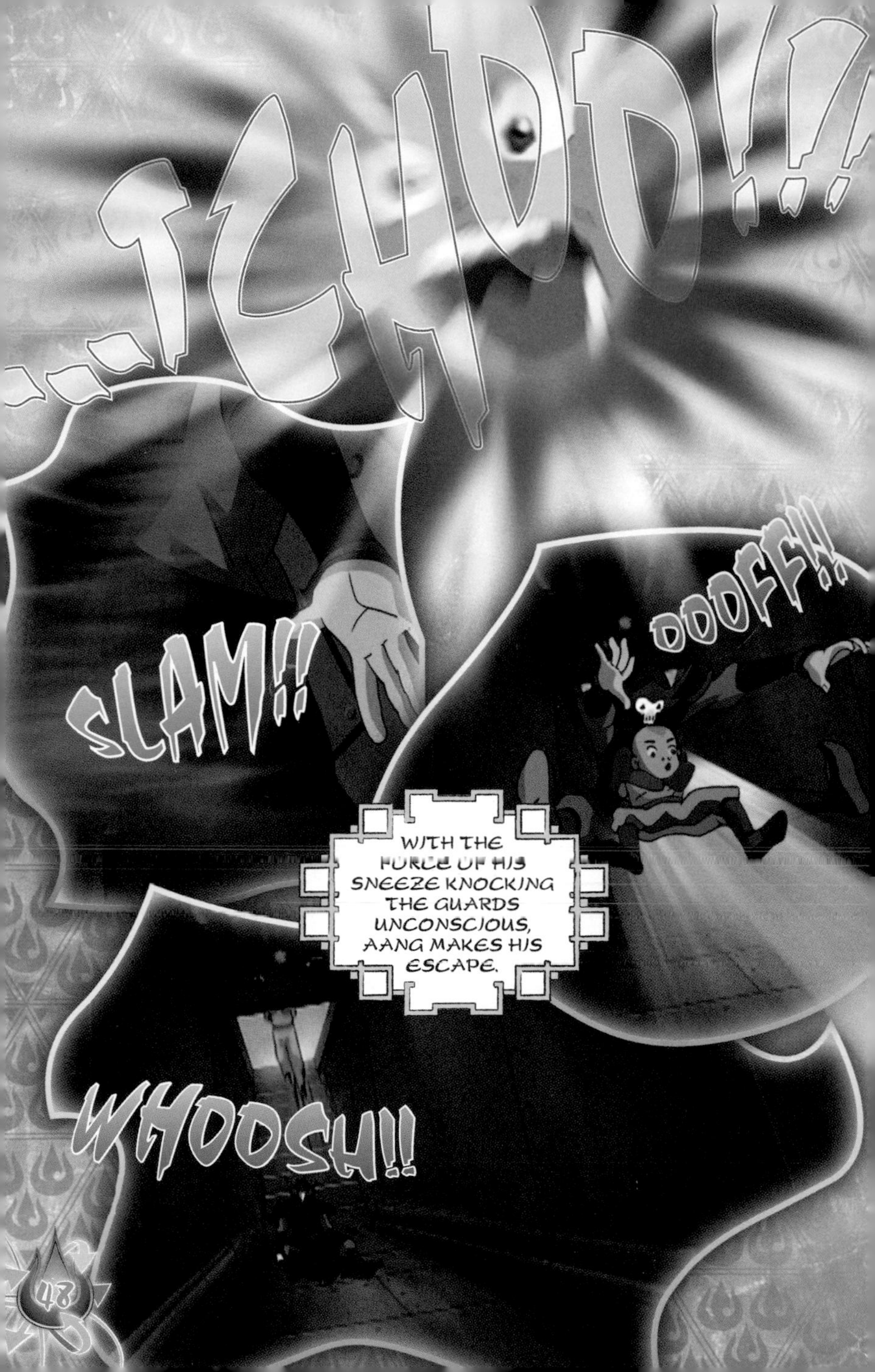
...TCHOO!!
SLAM!!
OOOFF!!
WITH THE FORCE OF HIS SNEEZE KNOCKING THE GUARDS UNCONSCIOUS, AANG MAKES HIS ESCAPE.
WHOOSH!!

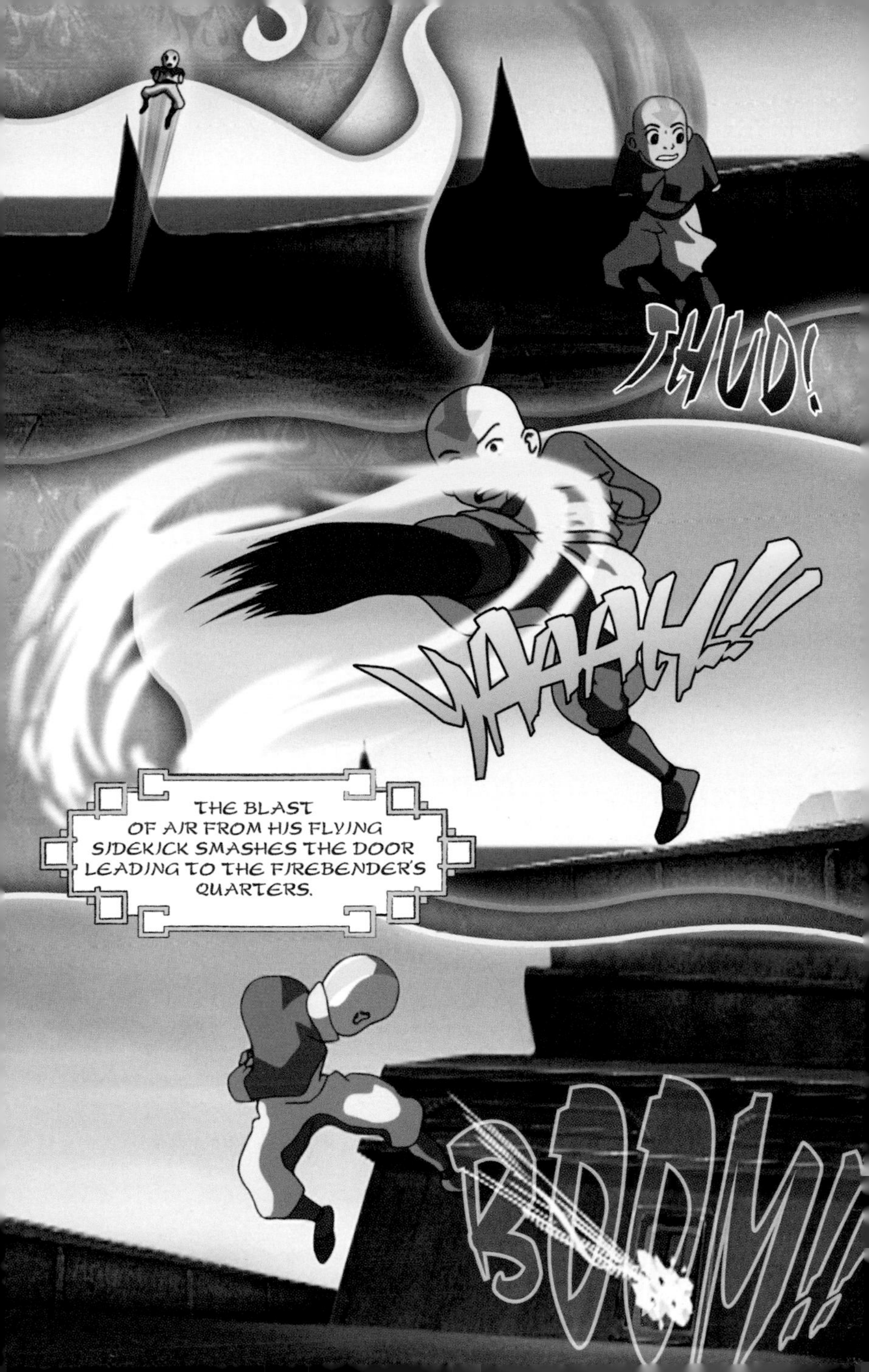
THUD!
YAAAH!!
THE BLAST OF AIR FROM HIS FLYING SIDEKICK SMASHES THE DOOR LEADING TO THE FIREBENDER'S QUARTERS.
BOOM!!

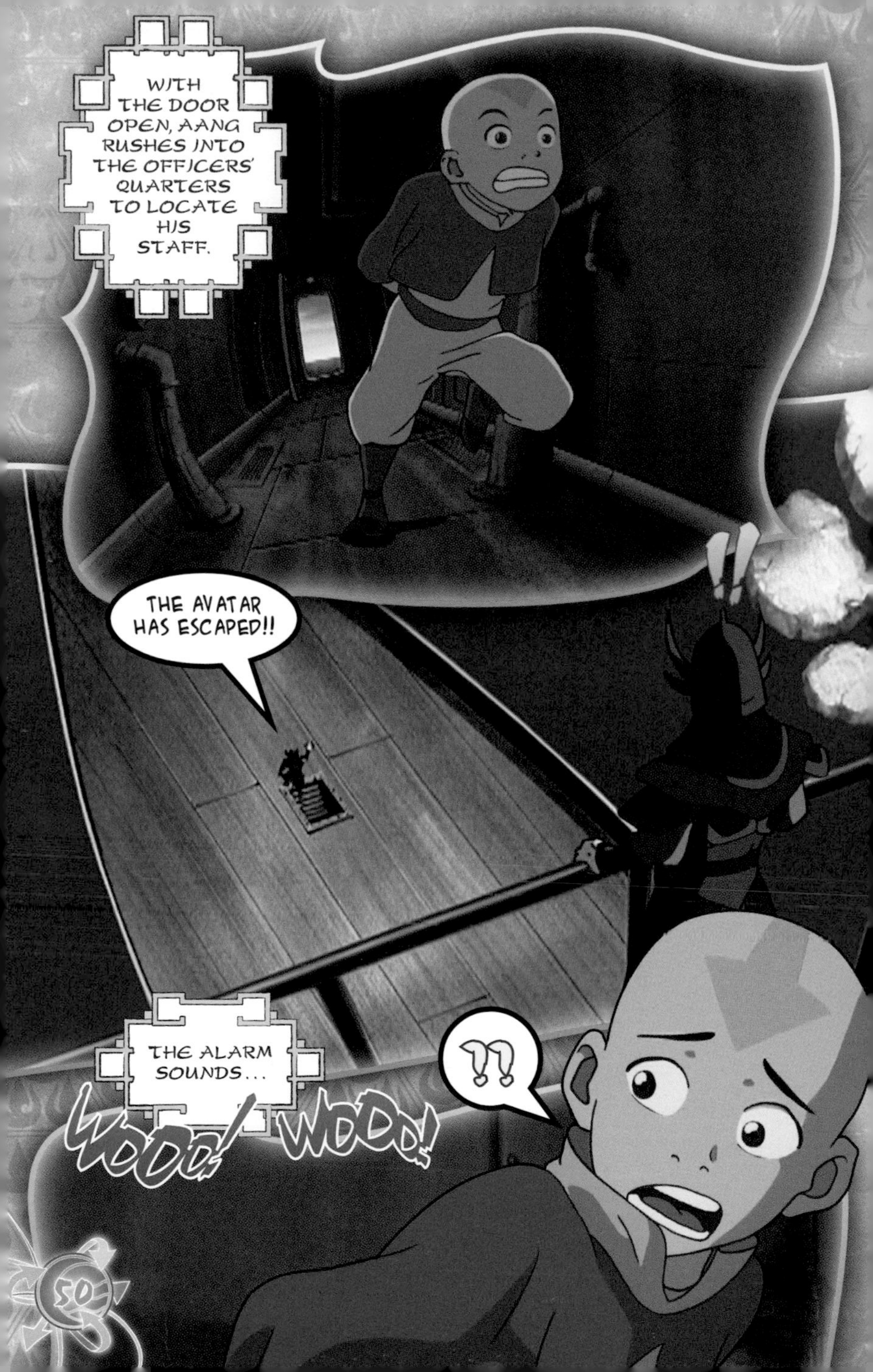
WITH THE DOOR OPEN, AANG RUSHES INTO THE OFFICERS' QUARTERS TO LOCATE HIS STAFF.
THE AVATAR HAS ESCAPED!!
THE ALARM SOUNDS...
WOOO! WOOO!
!!

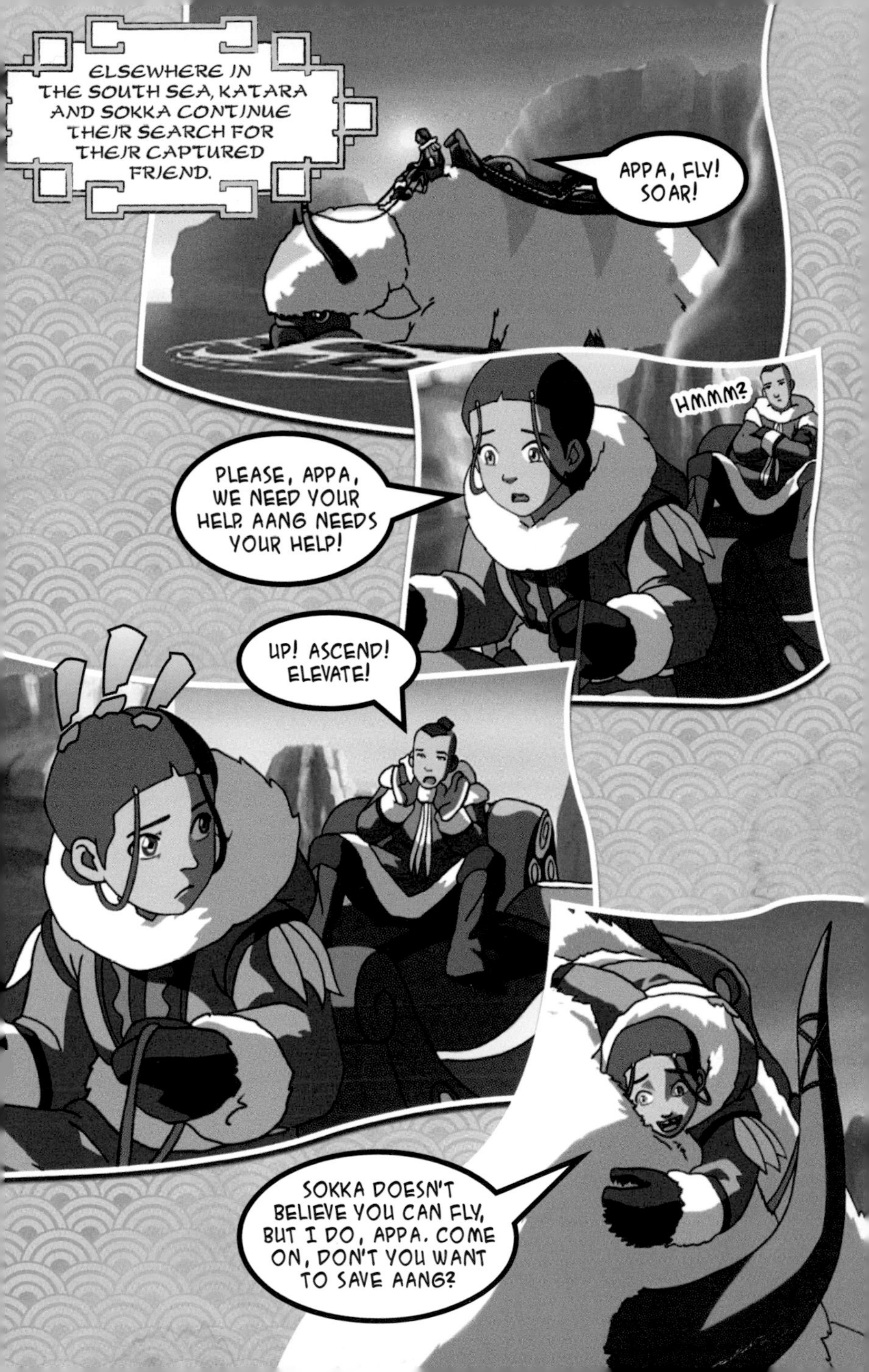
ELSEWHERE IN THE SOUTH SEA, KATARA AND SOKKA CONTINUE THEIR SEARCH FOR THEIR CAPTURED FRIEND.
APPA, FLY! SOAR!
PLEASE, APPA, WE NEED YOUR HELP. AANG NEEDS YOUR HELP!
HMMM?
UP! ASCEND! ELEVATE!
SOKKA DOESN'T BELIEVE YOU CAN FLY, BUT I DO, APPA. COME ON, DON'T YOU WANT TO SAVE AANG?

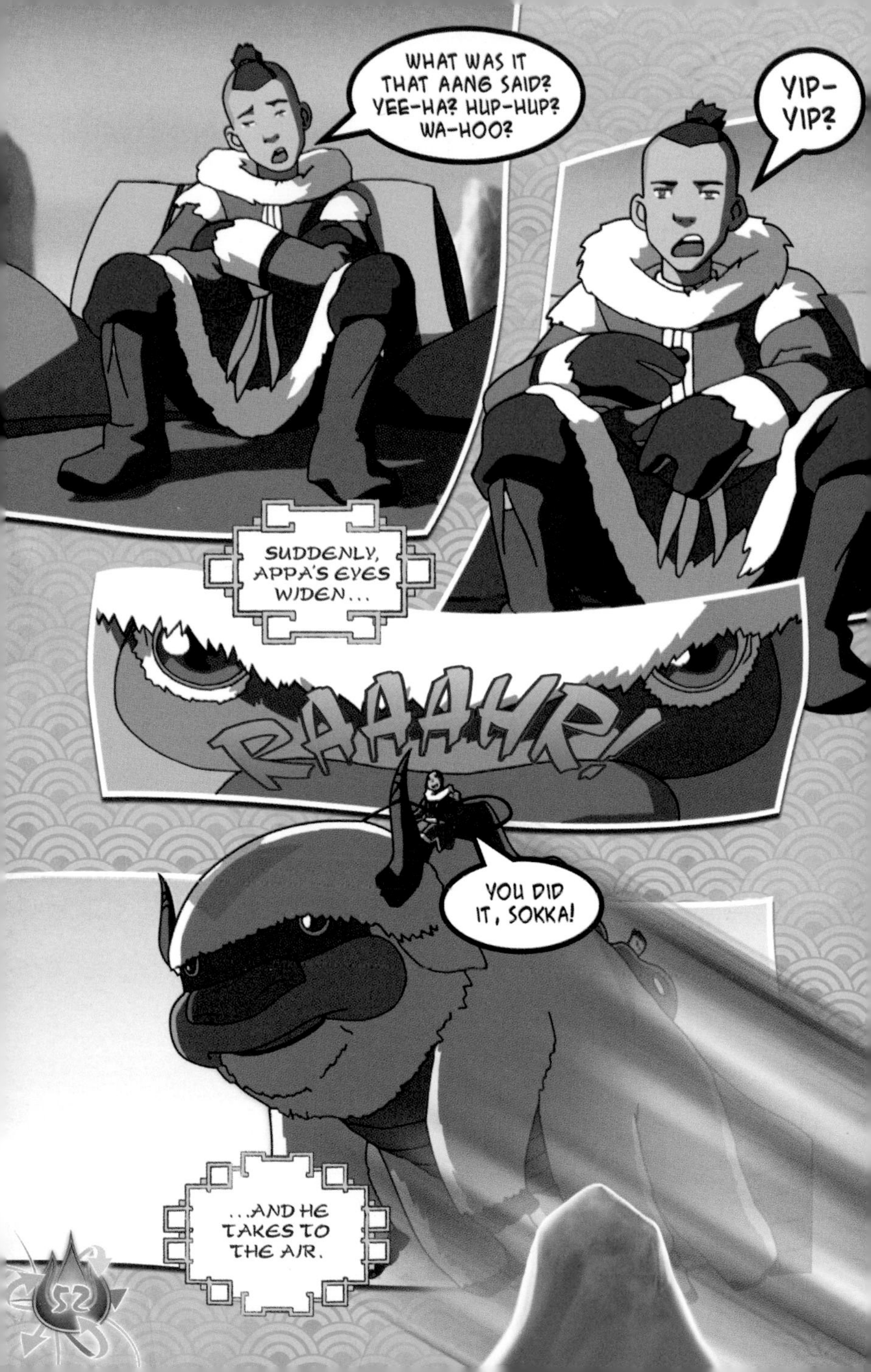
WHAT WAS IT THAT AANG SAID? YEE-HA? HUP-HUP? WA-HOO?
YIP-YIP?
SUDDENLY, APPA'S EYES WIDEN...
RAAAHR!
YOU DID IT, SOKKA!
...AND HE TAKES TO THE AIR.

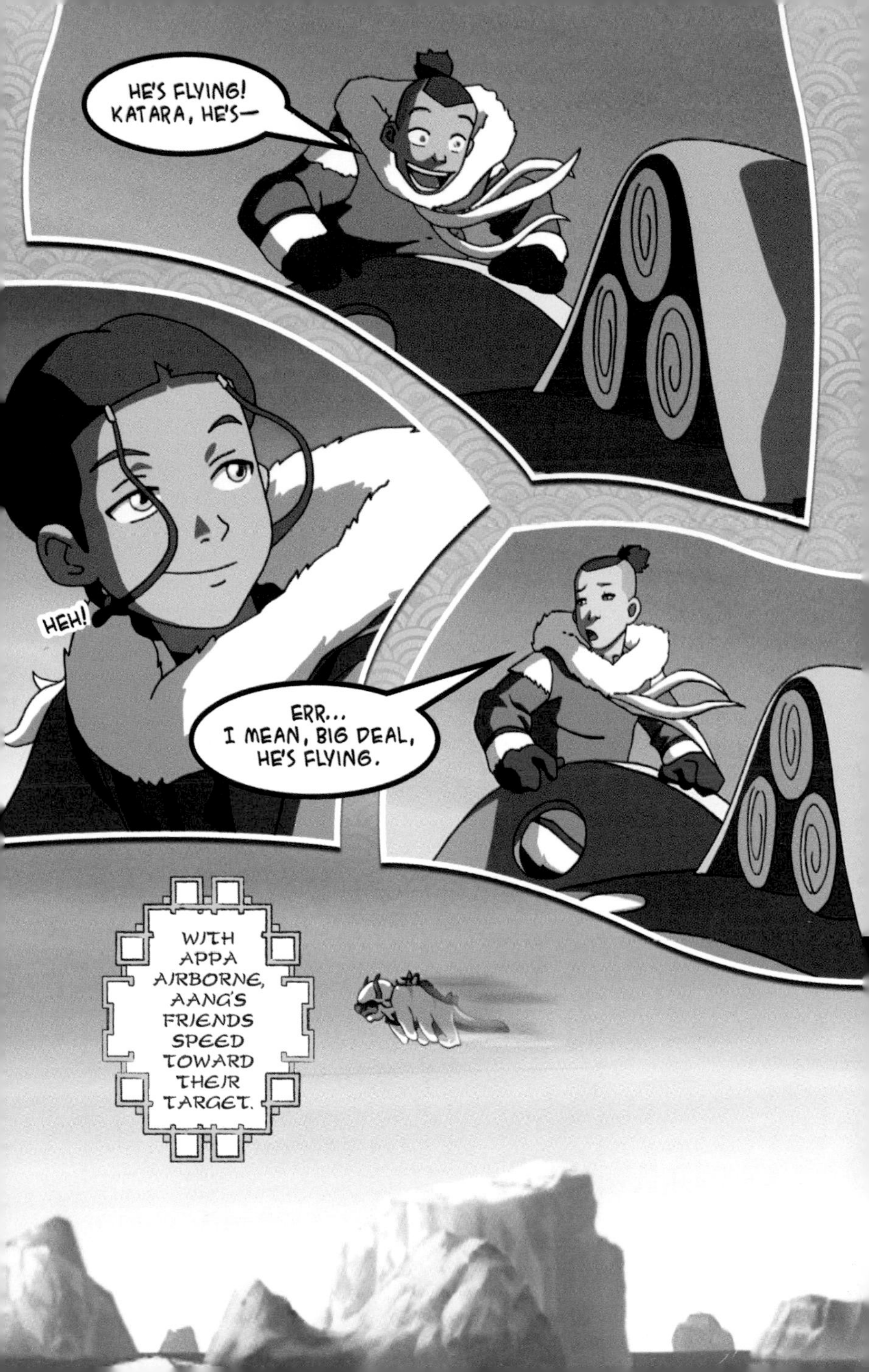
HE'S FLYING! KATARA, HE'S—
HEH!
ERR... I MEAN, BIG DEAL, HE'S FLYING.
WITH APPA AIRBORNE, AANG'S FRIENDS SPEED TOWARD THEIR TARGET.

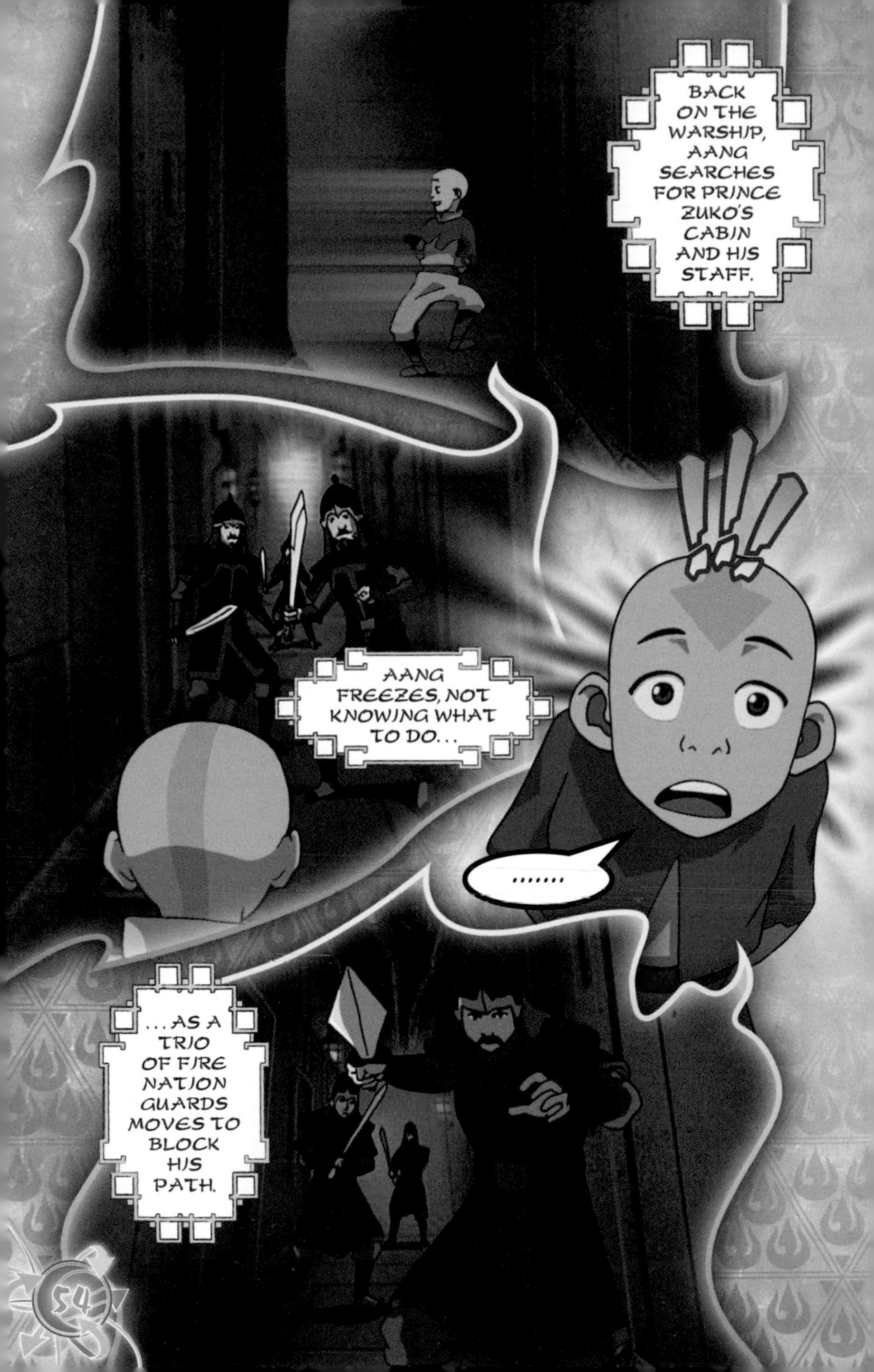
BACK ON THE WARSHIP, AANG SEARCHES FOR PRINCE ZUKO'S CABIN AND HIS STAFF.
AANG FREEZES, NOT KNOWING WHAT TO DO...
....
...AS A TRIO OF FIRE NATION GUARDS MOVES TO BLOCK HIS PATH.

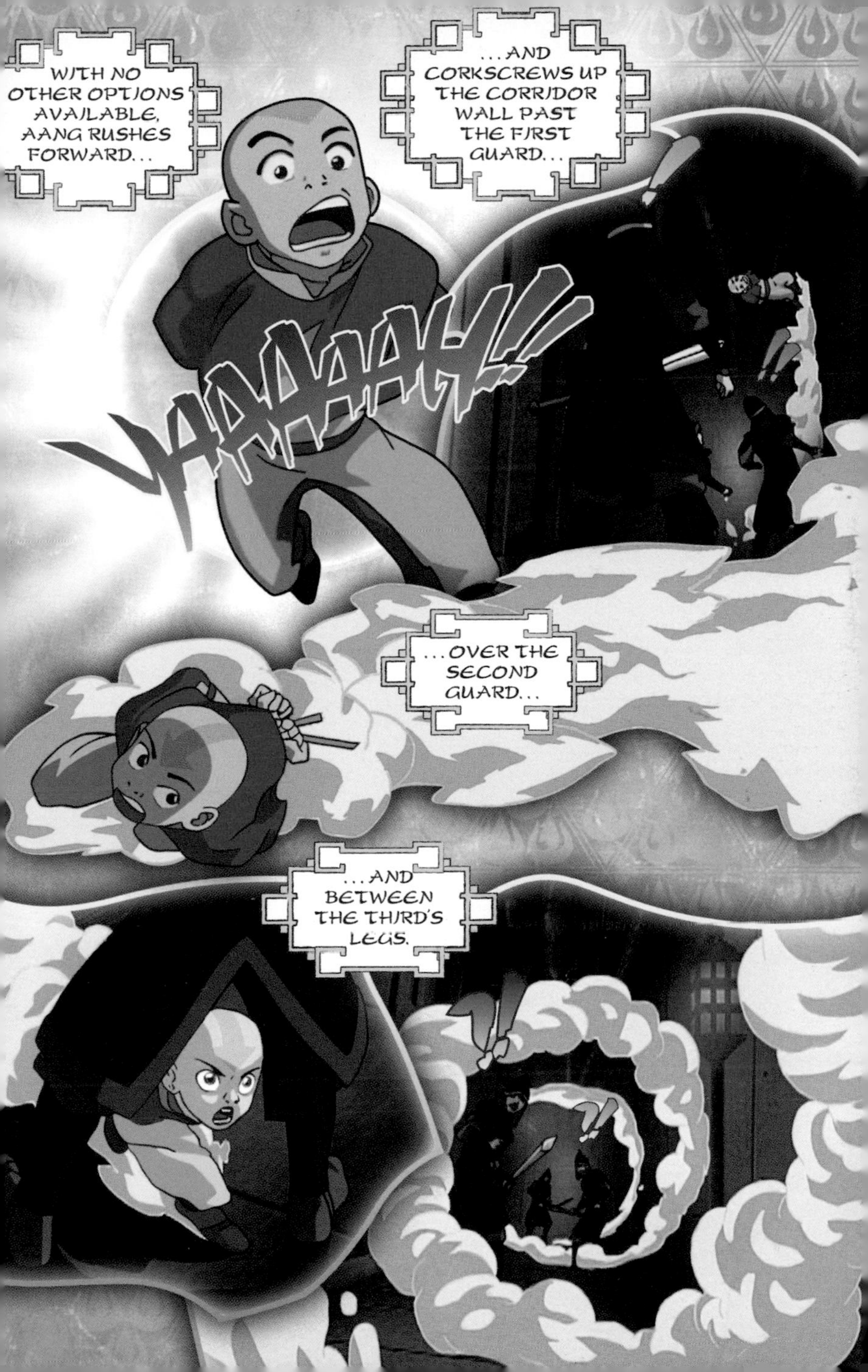
WITH NO OTHER OPTIONS AVAILABLE, AANG RUSHES FORWARD...
YAAAAAH!!
...AND CORKSCREWS UP THE CORRIDOR WALL PAST THE FIRST GUARD...
...OVER THE SECOND GUARD...
...AND BETWEEN THE THIRD'S LEGS.

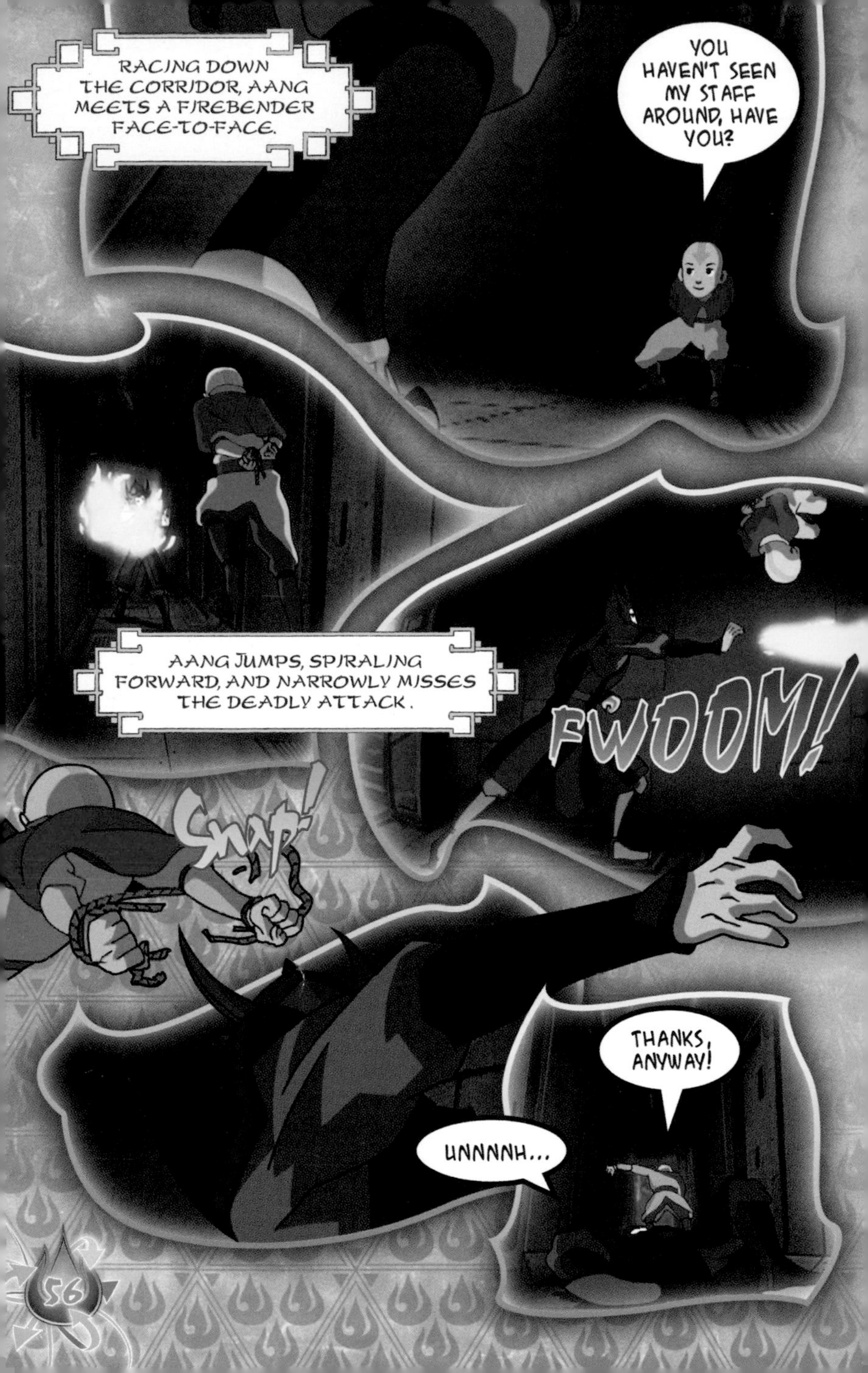
RACING DOWN THE CORRIDOR, AANG MEETS A FIREBENDER FACE-TO-FACE.
YOU HAVEN'T SEEN MY STAFF AROUND, HAVE YOU?
AANG JUMPS, SPIRALING FORWARD, AND NARROWLY MISSES THE DEADLY ATTACK.
FWOOM!
SNAP!
THANKS, ANYWAY!
UNNNNH...

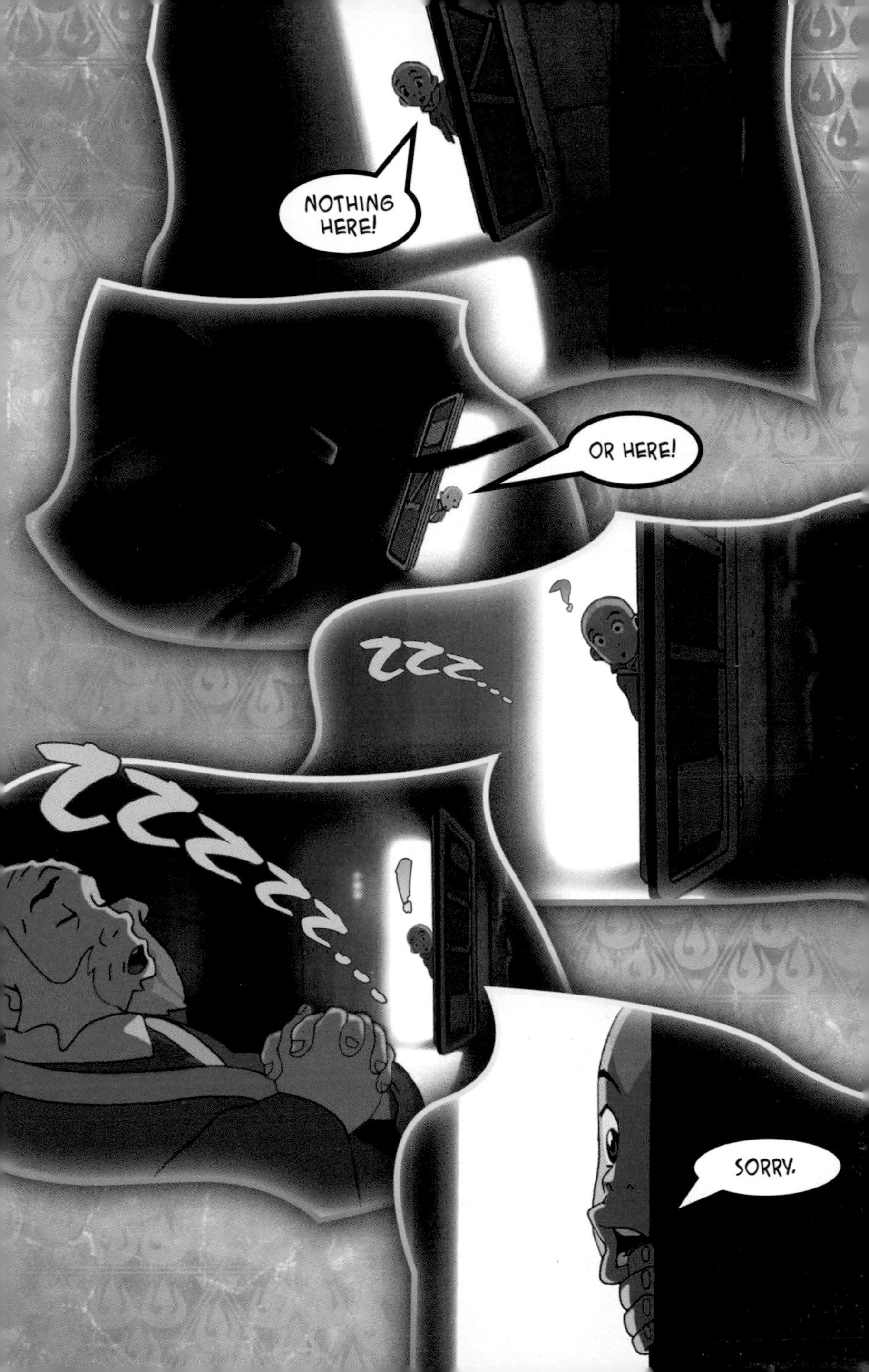
NOTHING HERE!
OR HERE!
ZZZ...
ZZZZZ...
!
SORRY.

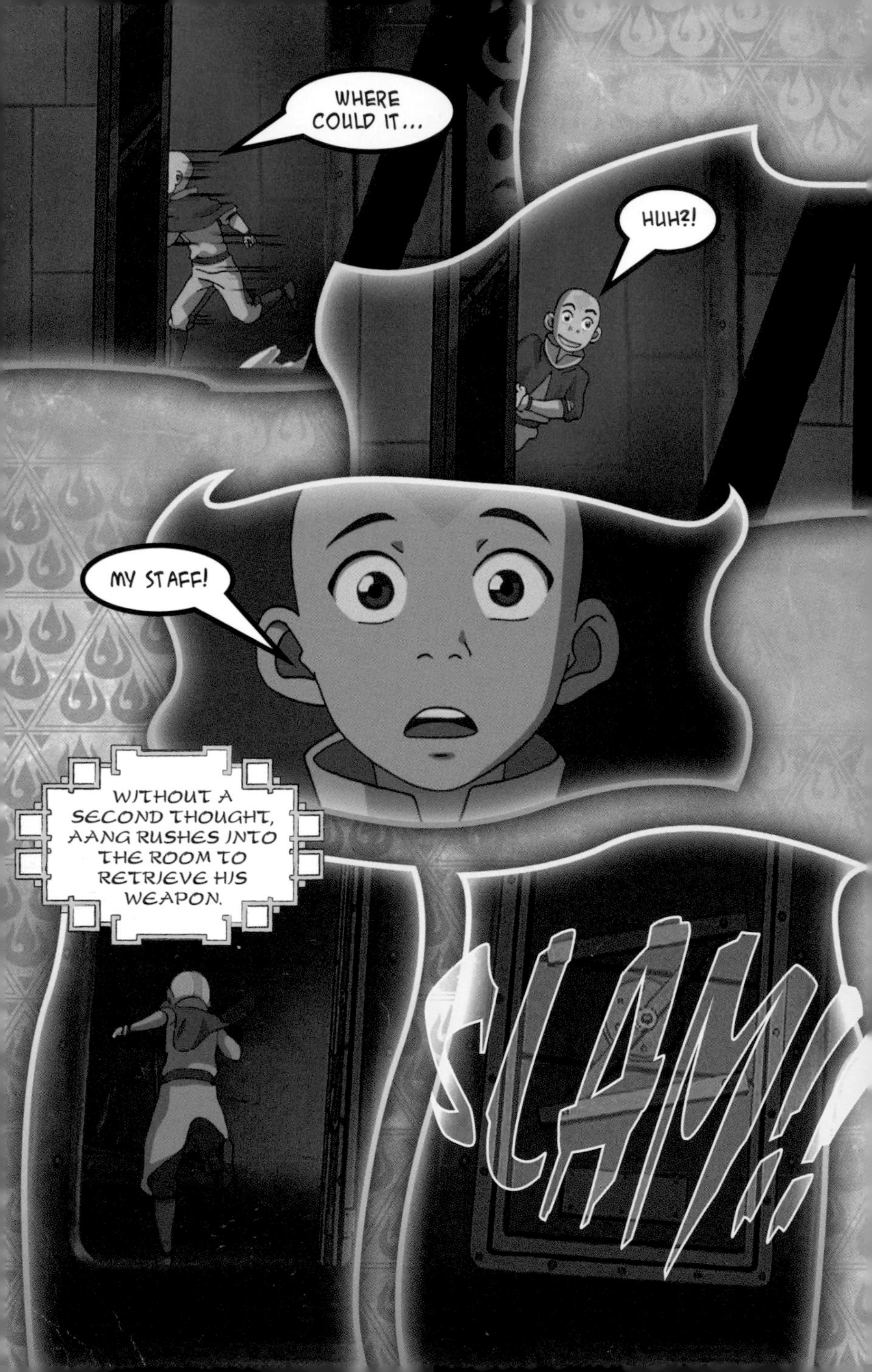
WHERE COULD IT...
HUH?!
MY STAFF!
WITHOUT A SECOND THOUGHT, AANG RUSHES INTO THE ROOM TO RETRIEVE HIS WEAPON.
SLAM!!

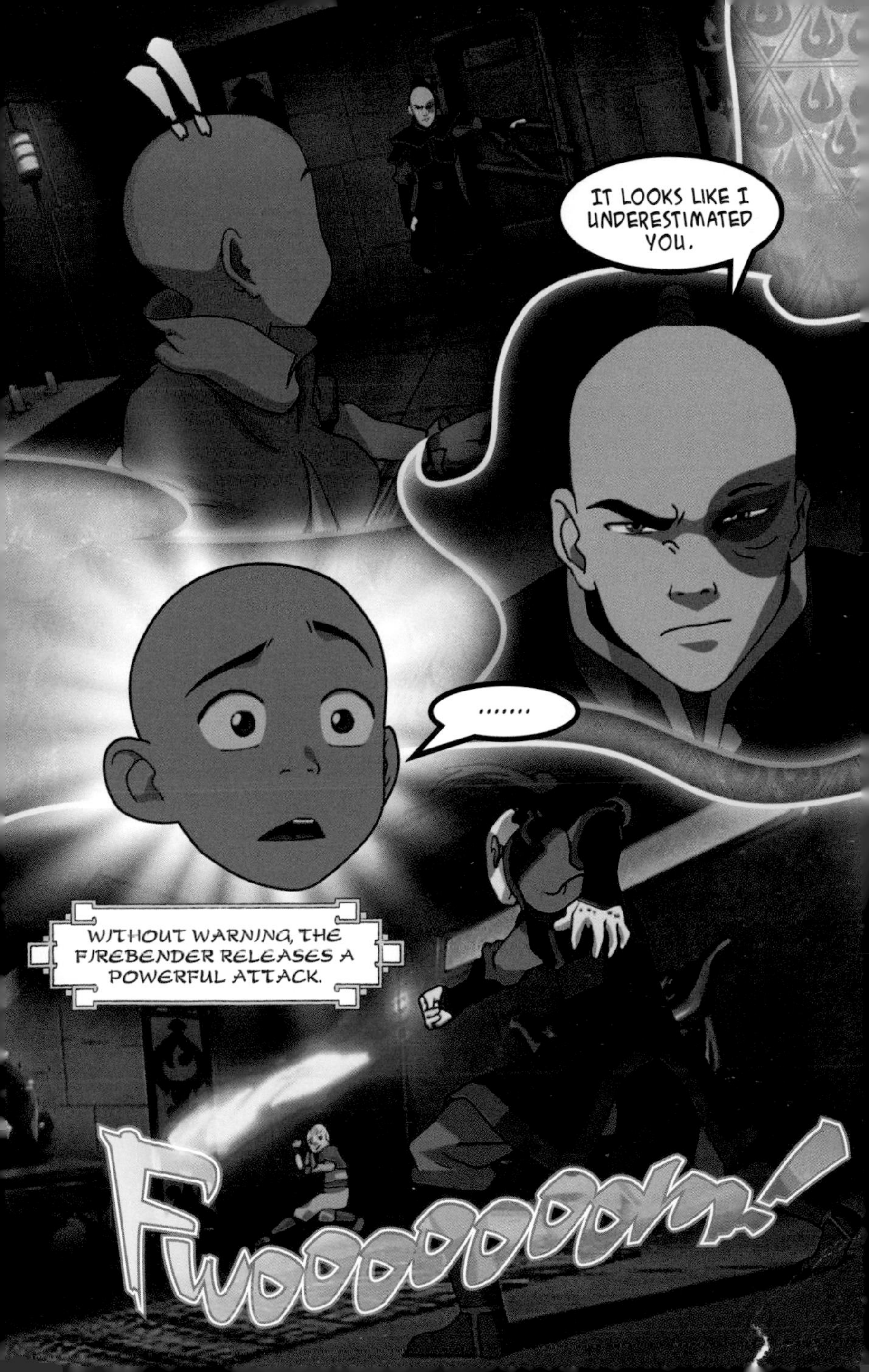
IT LOOKS LIKE I UNDERESTIMATED YOU.
....
WITHOUT WARNING, THE FIREBENDER RELEASES A POWERFUL ATTACK.
FWOOOOOOOM!

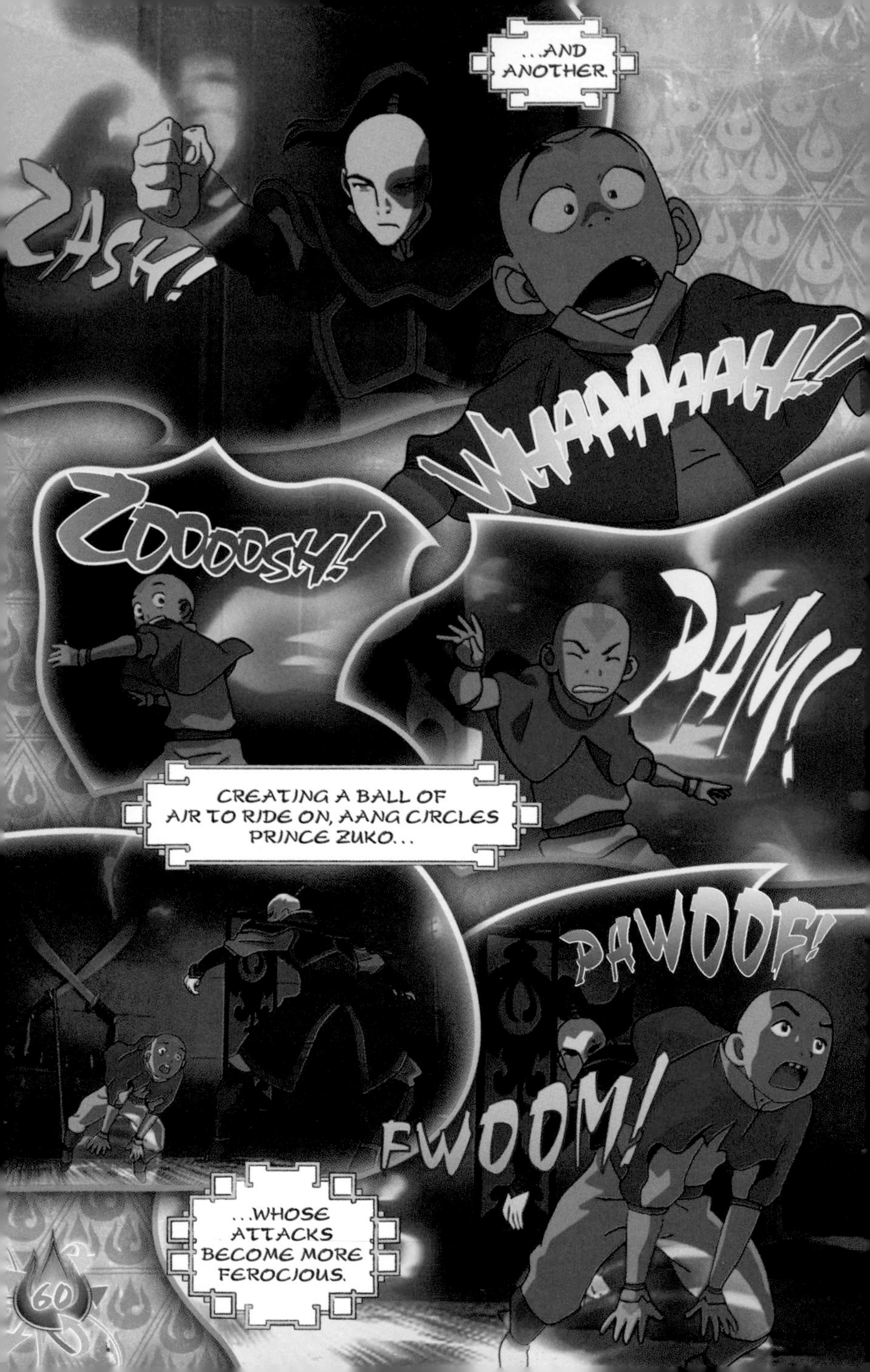
...AND ANOTHER.
ZASH!
WHAAAAAH!!
ZOOOOSH!
PAM!
CREATING A BALL OF AIR TO RIDE ON, AANG CIRCLES PRINCE ZUKO...
PAWOOF!
FWOOM!
...WHOSE ATTACKS BECOME MORE FEROCIOUS.

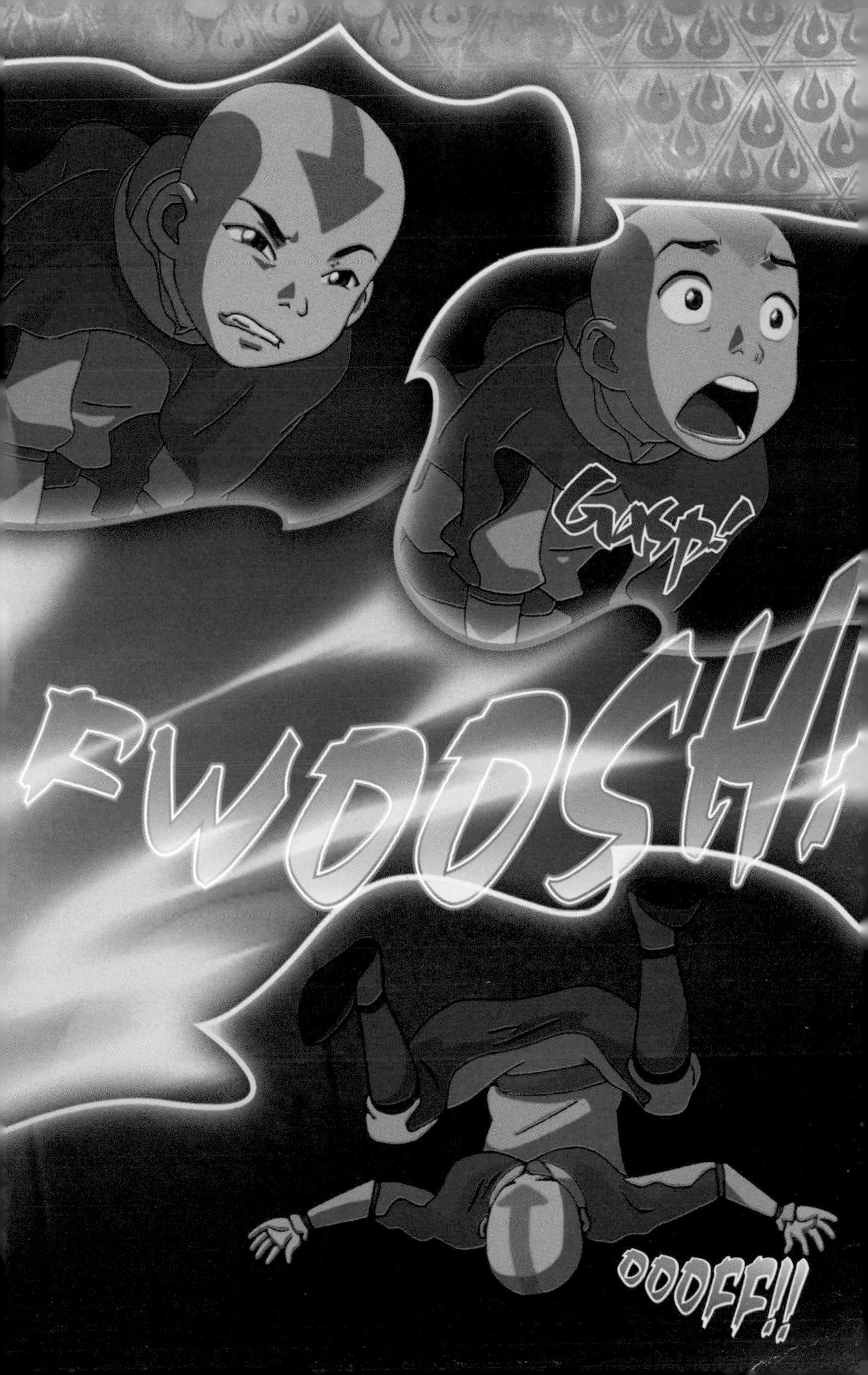
Gasp!
FWOOSH!
OOOFF!!

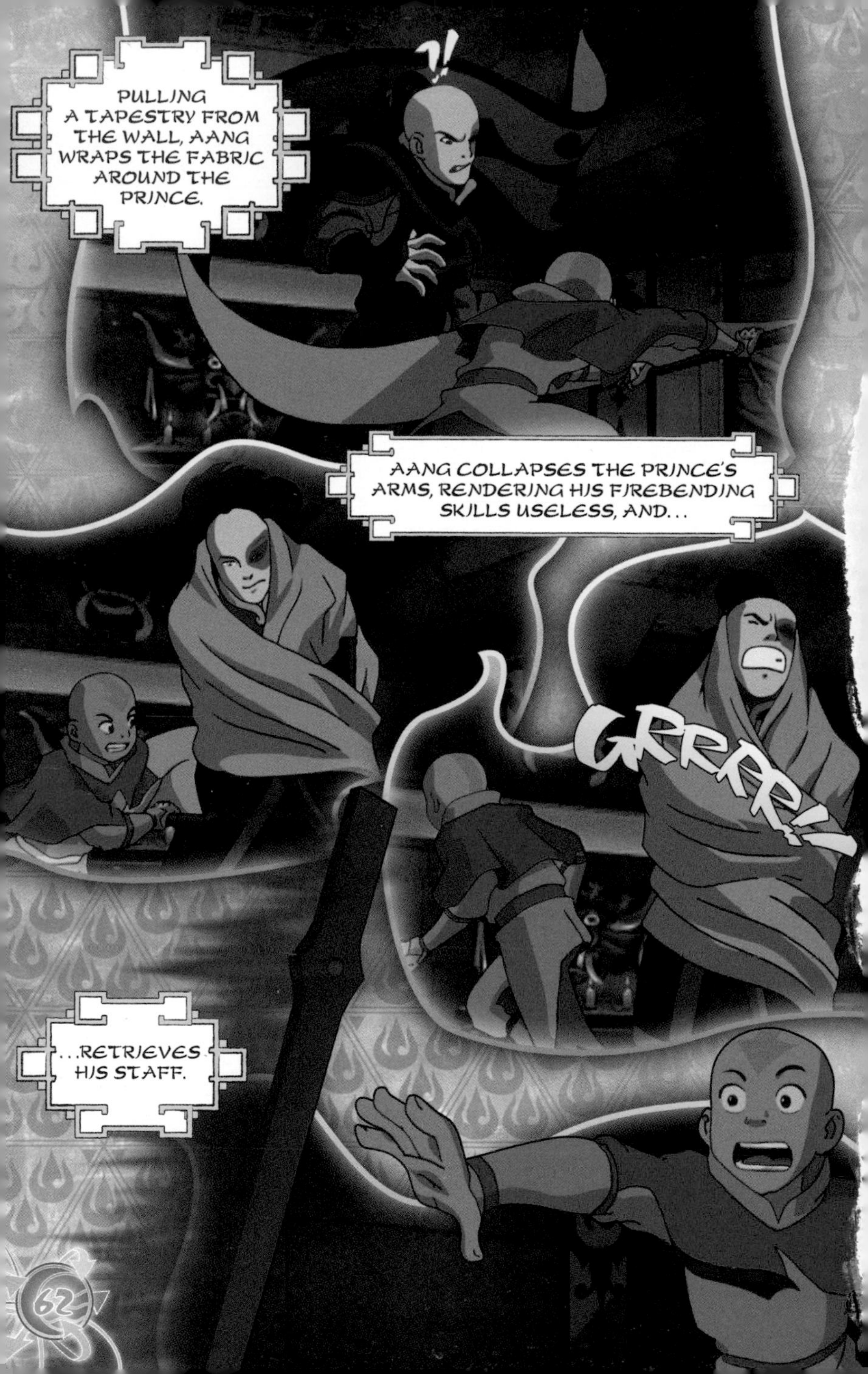
PULLING A TAPESTRY FROM THE WALL, AANG WRAPS THE FABRIC AROUND THE PRINCE.
?!
AANG COLLAPSES THE PRINCE'S ARMS, RENDERING HIS FIREBENDING SKILLS USELESS, AND. . .
GRRRR!!
. . .RETRIEVES HIS STAFF.

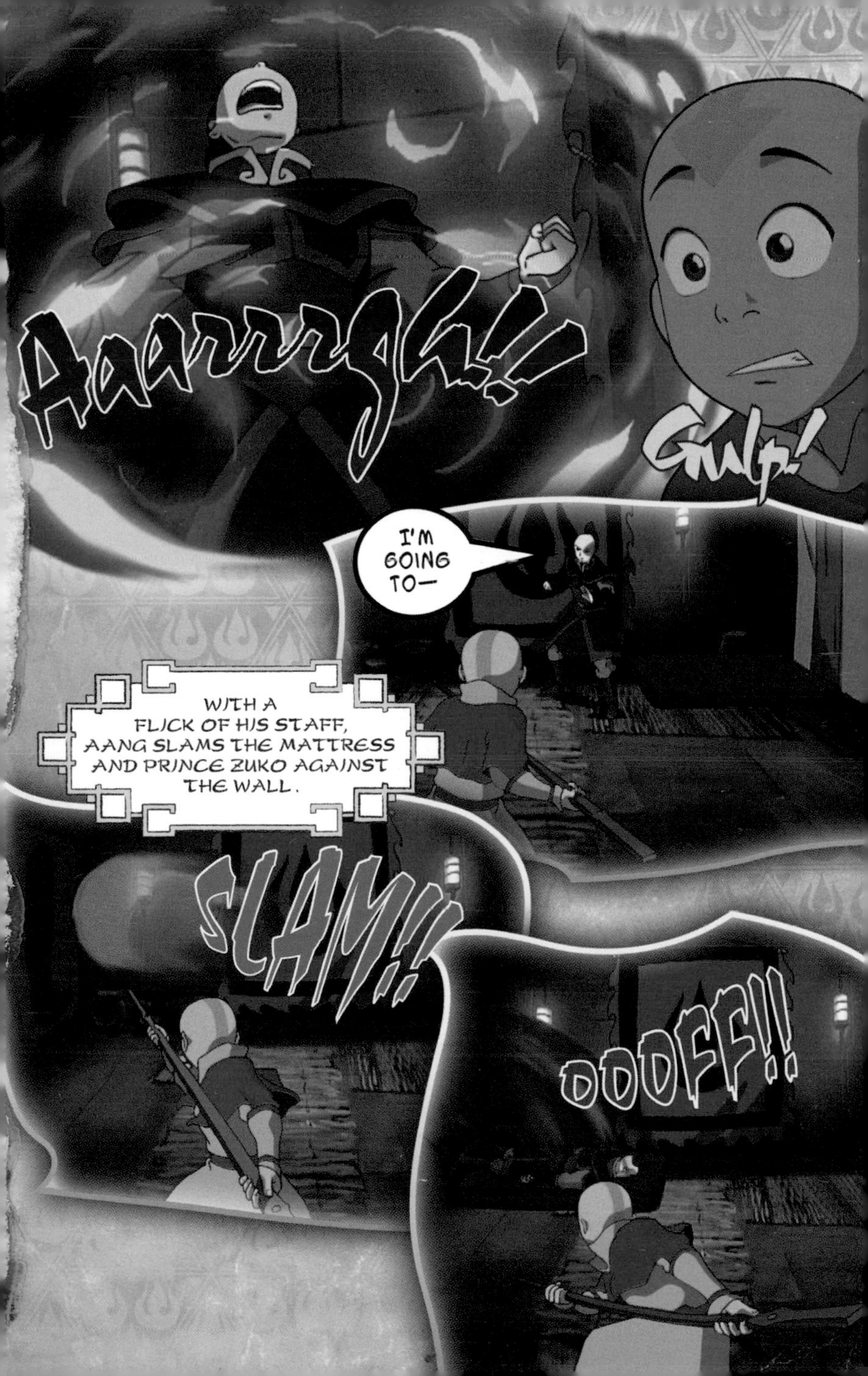
Aaarrrgh!!
Gulp!
I'M GOING TO—
WITH A FLICK OF HIS STAFF, AANG SLAMS THE MATTRESS AND PRINCE ZUKO AGAINST THE WALL.
SLAM!!
OOOFF!!

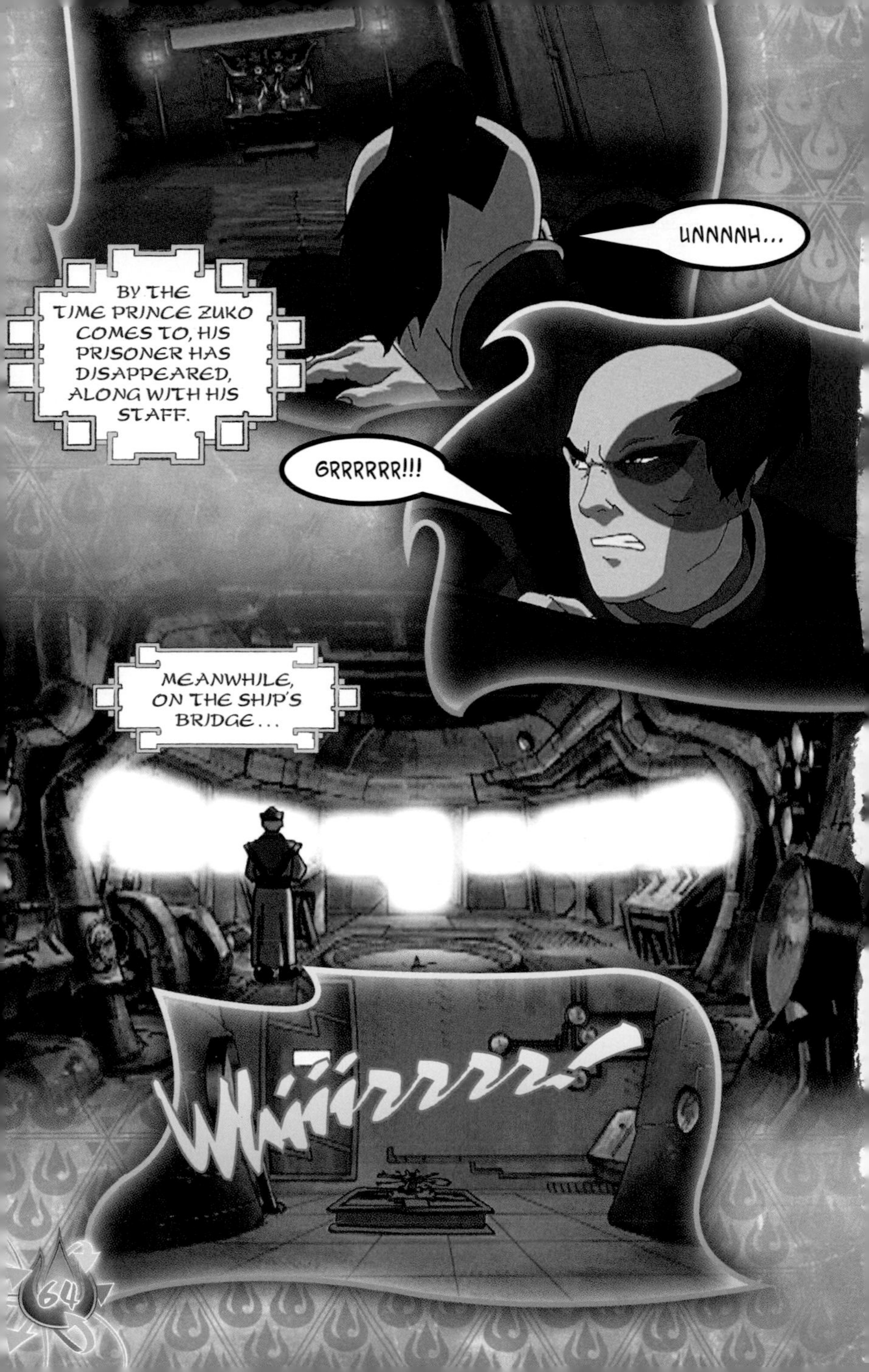
UNNNNH...
BY THE TIME PRINCE ZUKO COMES TO, HIS PRISONER HAS DISAPPEARED, ALONG WITH HIS STAFF.
GRRRRRR!!!
MEANWHILE, ON THE SHIP'S BRIDGE...
Whiirrrrr!

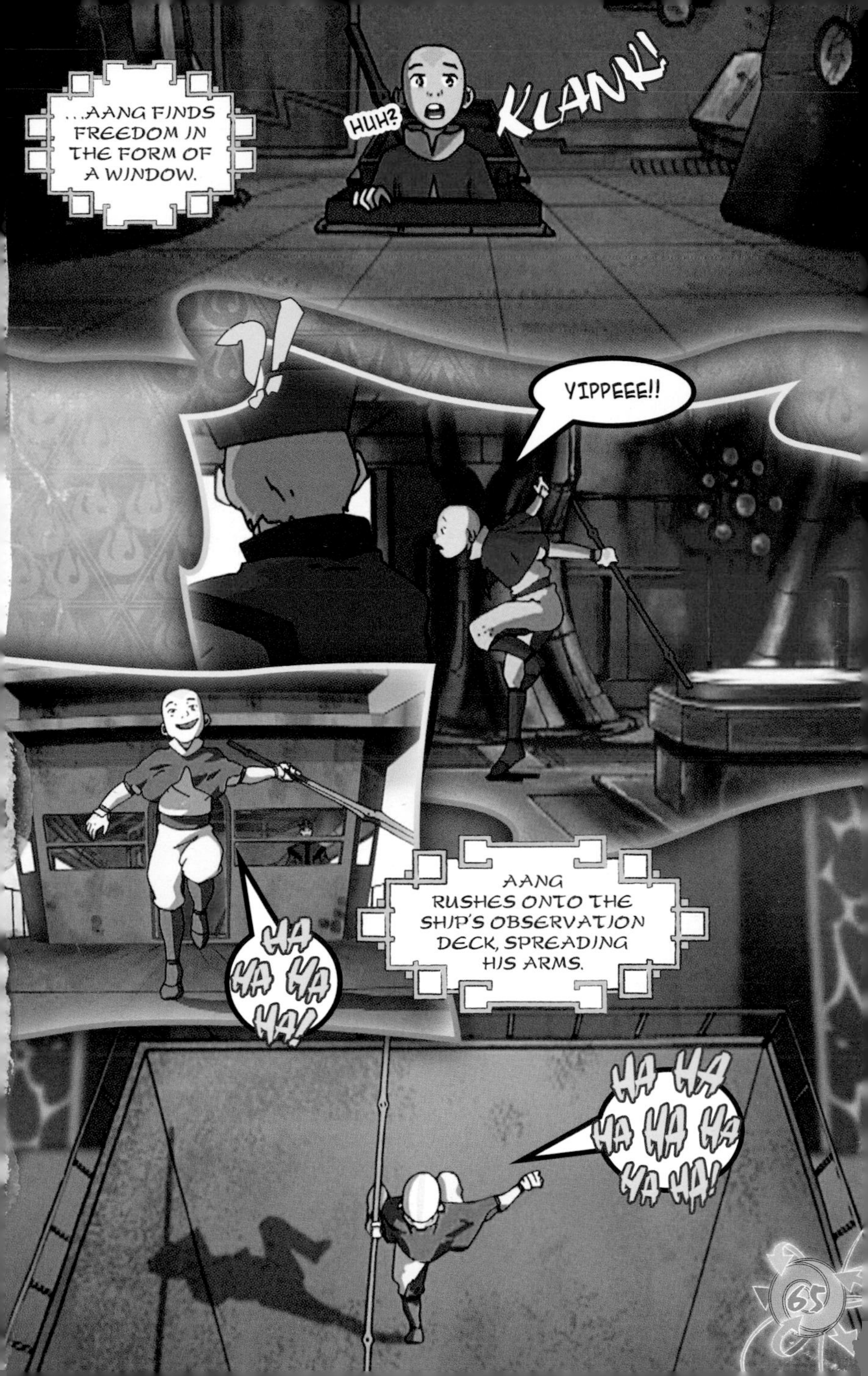
...AANG FINDS FREEDOM IN THE FORM OF A WINDOW.
HUH?
KLANK!
?!
YIPPEEE!!
HA HA HA HA!
AANG RUSHES ONTO THE SHIP'S OBSERVATION DECK, SPREADING HIS ARMS.
HA HA HA HA HA HA HA!
65

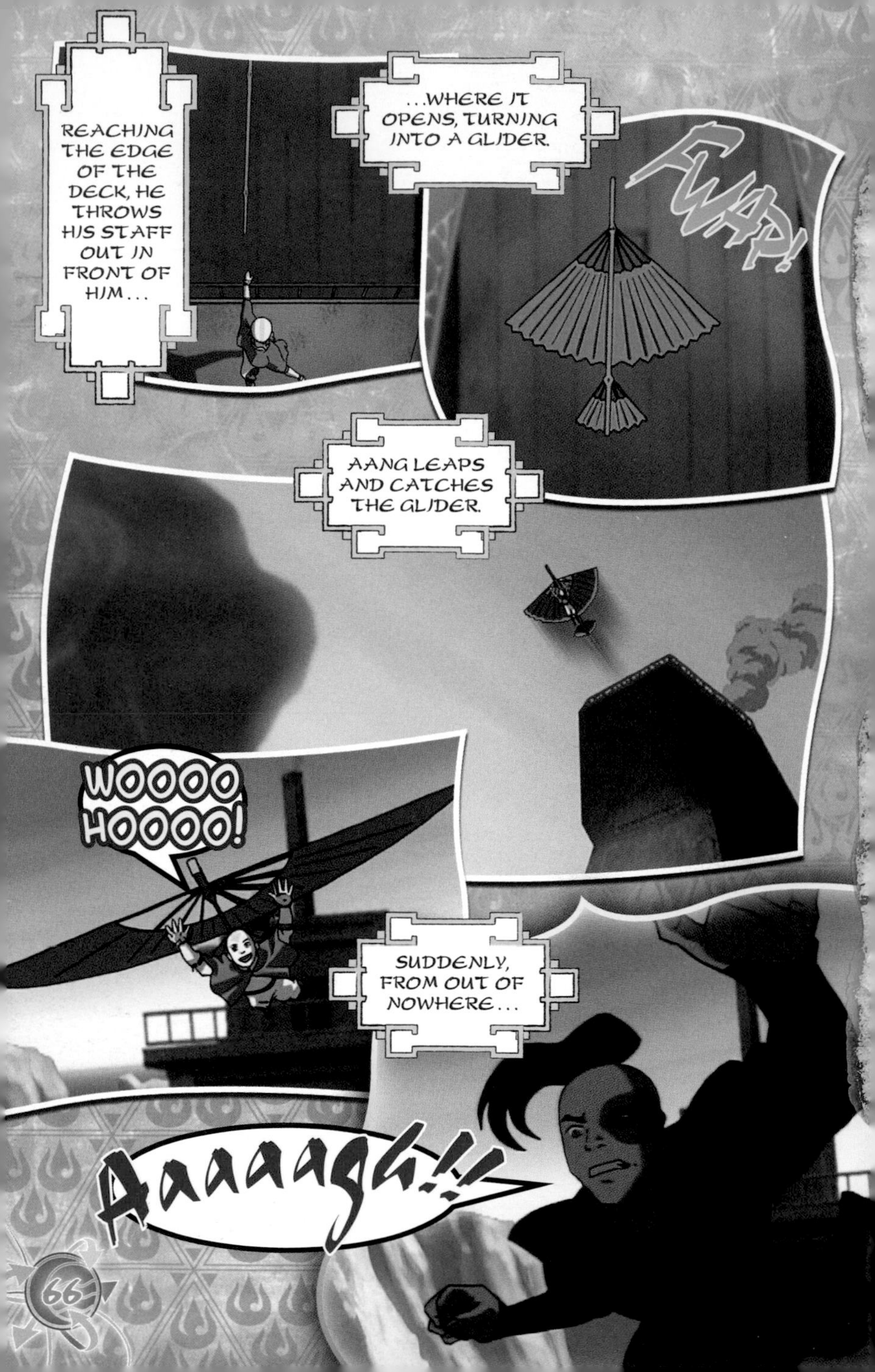
REACHING THE EDGE OF THE DECK, HE THROWS HIS STAFF OUT IN FRONT OF HIM . . .
. . . WHERE IT OPENS, TURNING INTO A GLIDER.
FWAP!
AANG LEAPS AND CATCHES THE GLIDER.
WOOOO HOOOO!
SUDDENLY, FROM OUT OF NOWHERE . . .
Aaaaagh!!

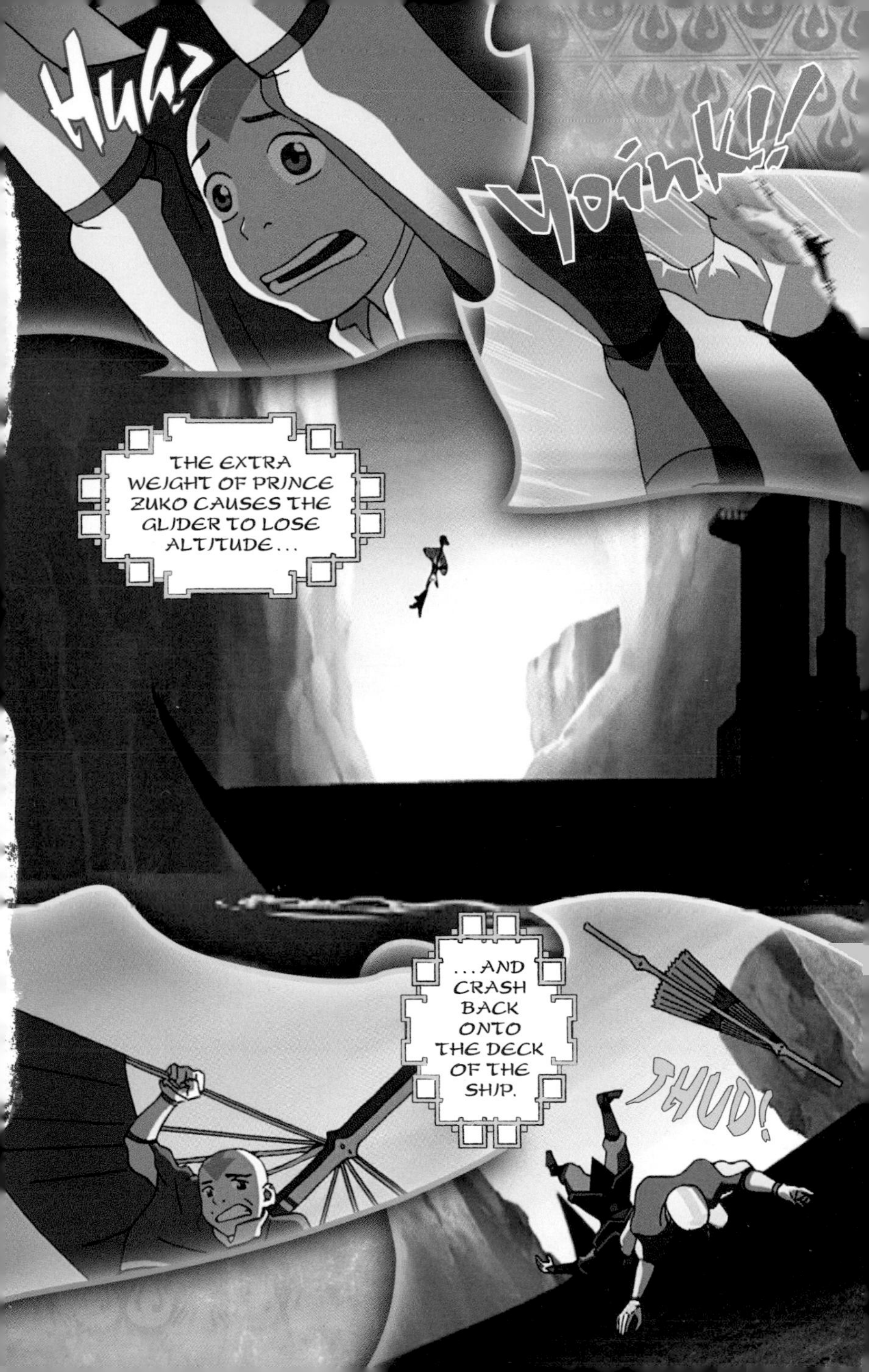
HUH?
YOINK!!
THE EXTRA WEIGHT OF PRINCE ZUKO CAUSES THE GLIDER TO LOSE ALTITUDE . . .
. . . AND CRASH BACK ONTO THE DECK OF THE SHIP.
THUD!

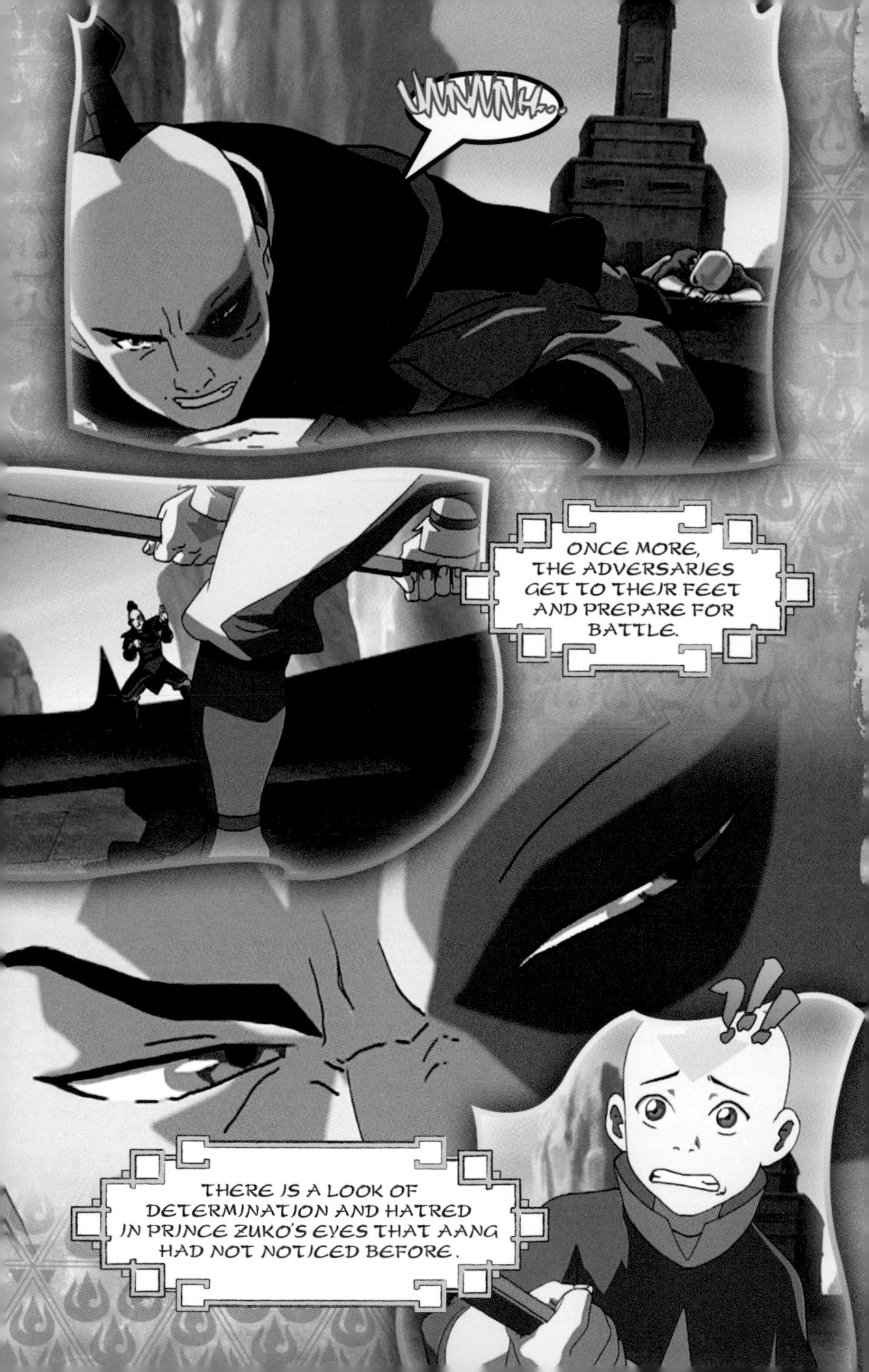
UNNNNH...
ONCE MORE, THE ADVERSARIES GET TO THEIR FEET AND PREPARE FOR BATTLE.
THERE IS A LOOK OF DETERMINATION AND HATRED IN PRINCE ZUKO'S EYES THAT AANG HAD NOT NOTICED BEFORE.

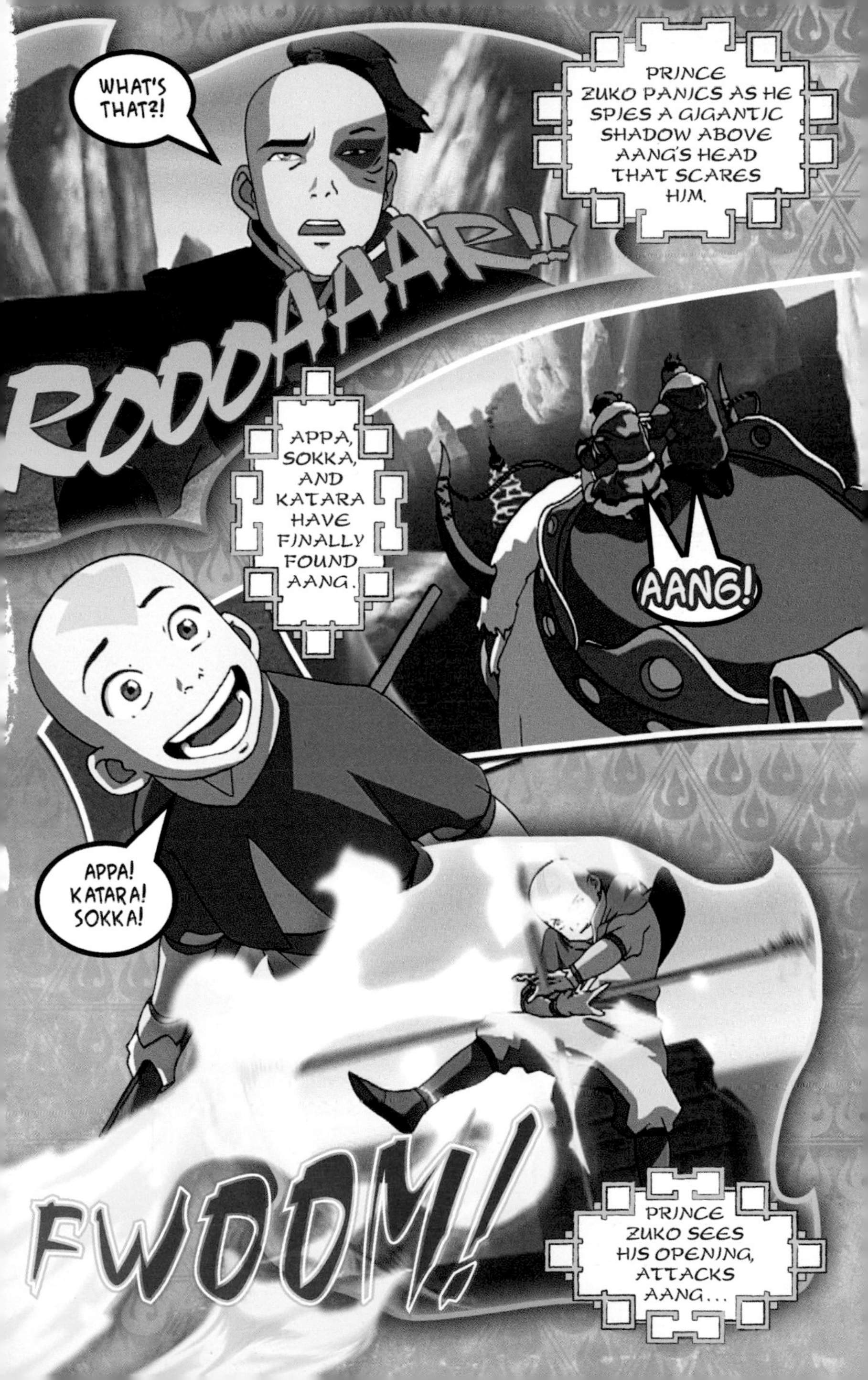
WHAT'S THAT?!
PRINCE ZUKO PANICS AS HE SPIES A GIGANTIC SHADOW ABOVE AANG'S HEAD THAT SCARES HIM.
ROOOAAAR!!
APPA, SOKKA, AND KATARA HAVE FINALLY FOUND AANG.
AANG!
APPA! KATARA! SOKKA!
FWOOM!
PRINCE ZUKO SEES HIS OPENING, ATTACKS AANG...

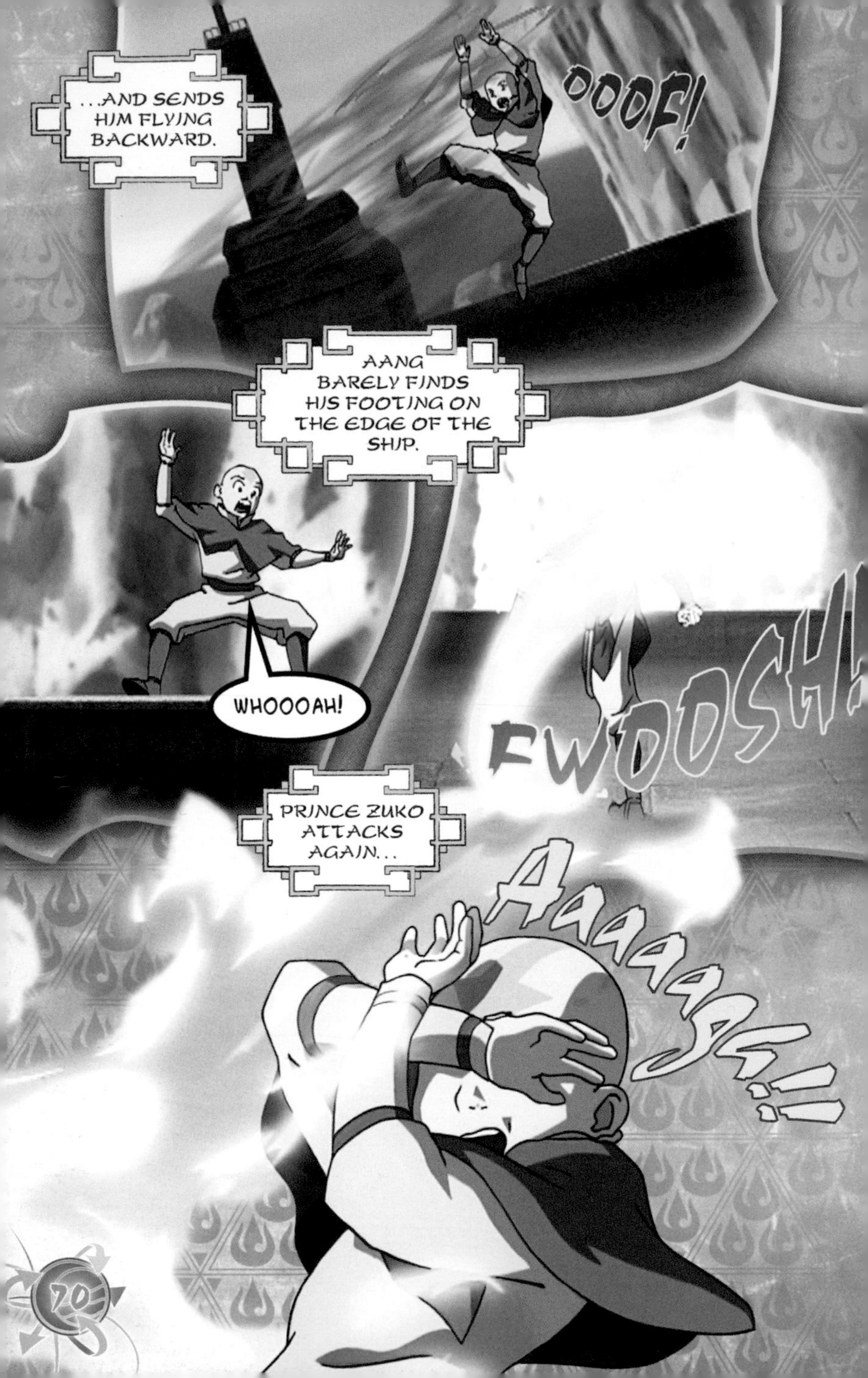

...AND SENDS HIM FLYING BACKWARD.
OOOOF!
AANG BARELY FINDS HIS FOOTING ON THE EDGE OF THE SHIP.
WHOOOAH!
FWOOSH!
PRINCE ZUKO ATTACKS AGAIN...
Aaaaagh!!!

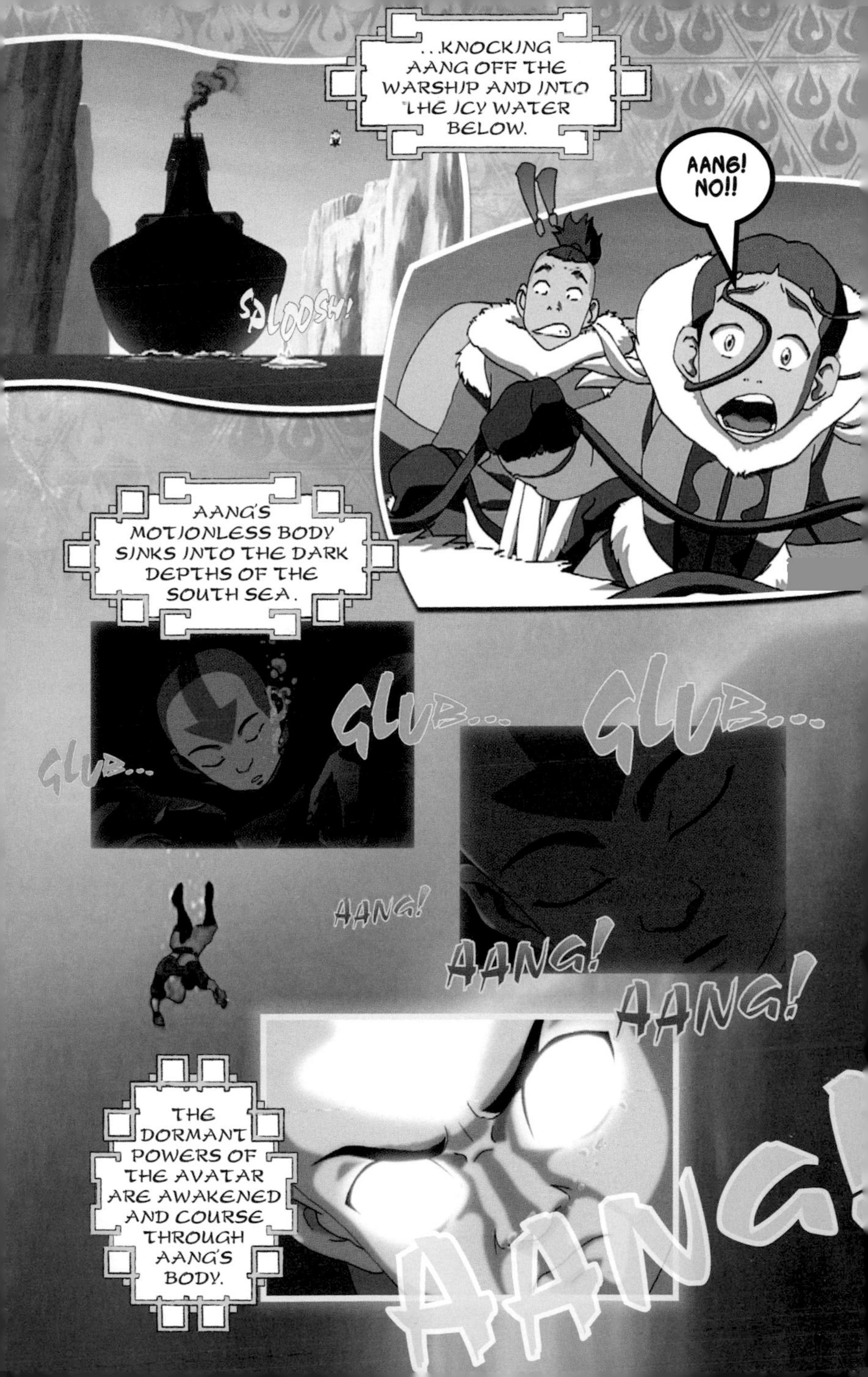
...KNOCKING AANG OFF THE WARSHIP AND INTO THE ICY WATER BELOW.
SPLOOSH!
AANG! NO!!
AANG'S MOTIONLESS BODY SINKS INTO THE DARK DEPTHS OF THE SOUTH SEA.
GLUB...
GLUB...
GLUB...
AANG!
AANG!
AANG!
THE DORMANT POWERS OF THE AVATAR ARE AWAKENED AND COURSE THROUGH AANG'S BODY.
AANG!

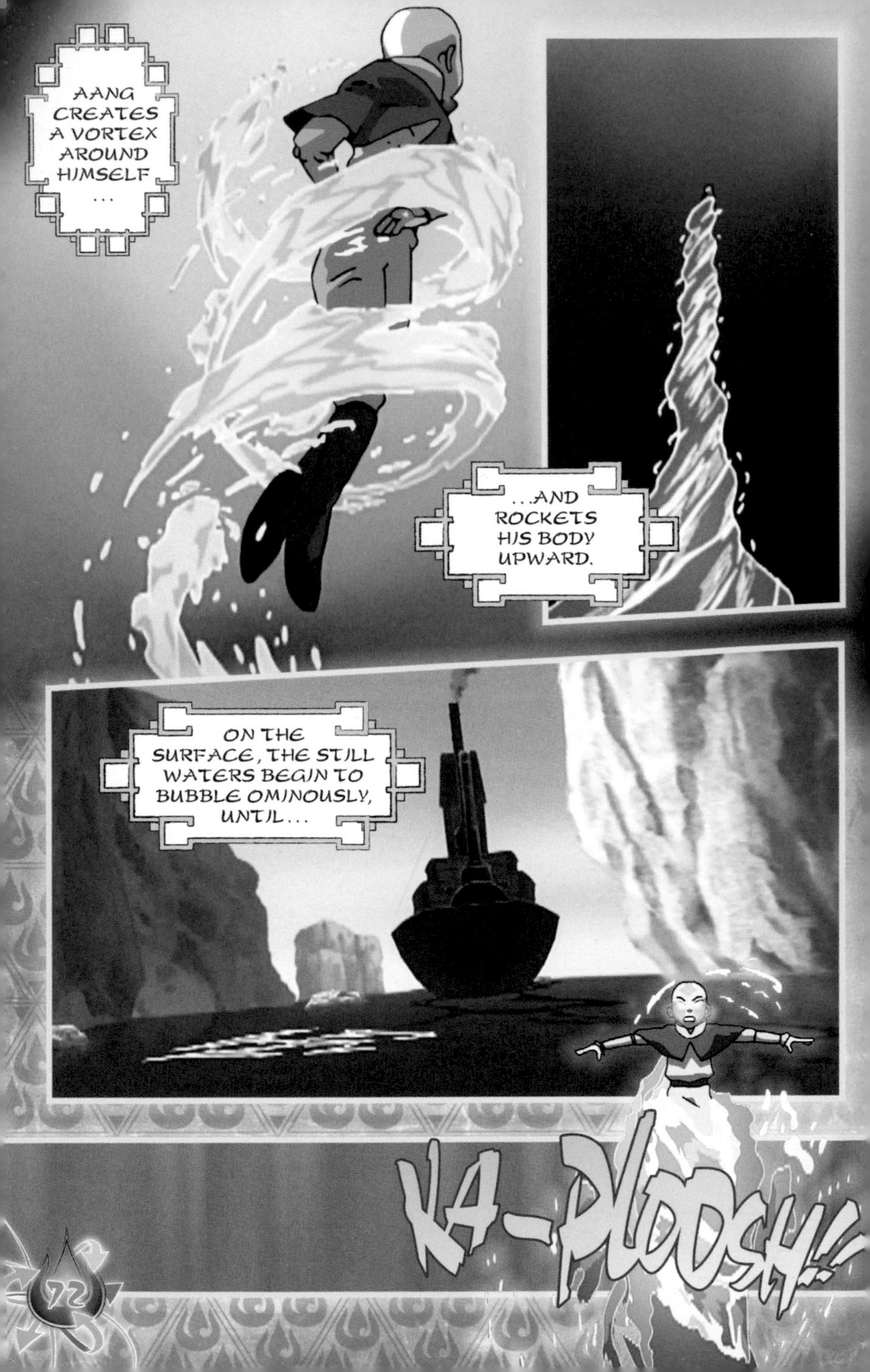
AANG CREATES A VORTEX AROUND HIMSELF . . .
. . .AND ROCKETS HIS BODY UPWARD.
ON THE SURFACE, THE STILL WATERS BEGIN TO BUBBLE OMINOUSLY, UNTIL . . .
KA-PLOOSH!!

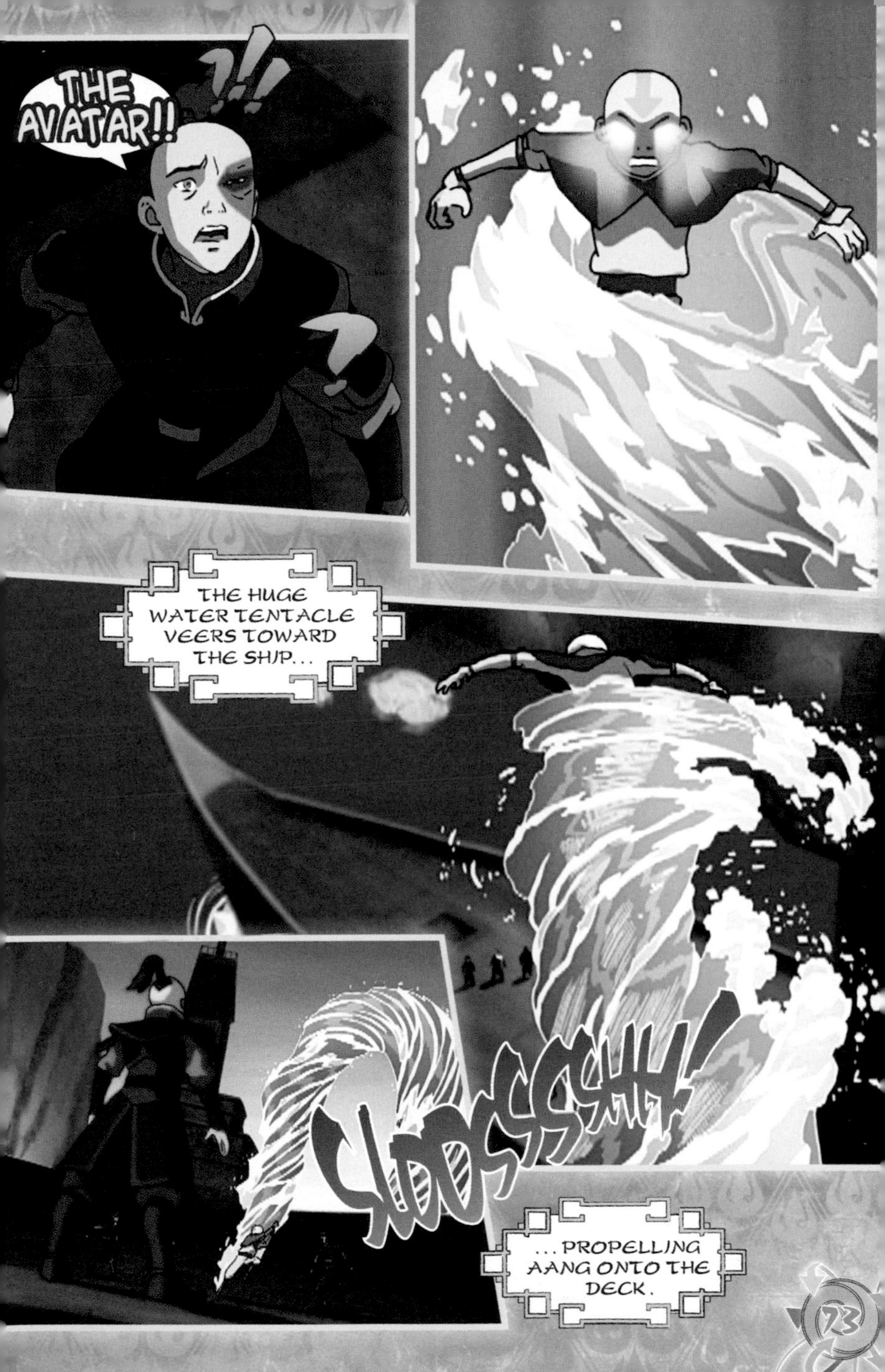
THE AVATAR!!
?!!
THE HUGE WATER TENTACLE VEERS TOWARD THE SHIP...
SLOOSSSHH!
...PROPELLING AANG ONTO THE DECK.

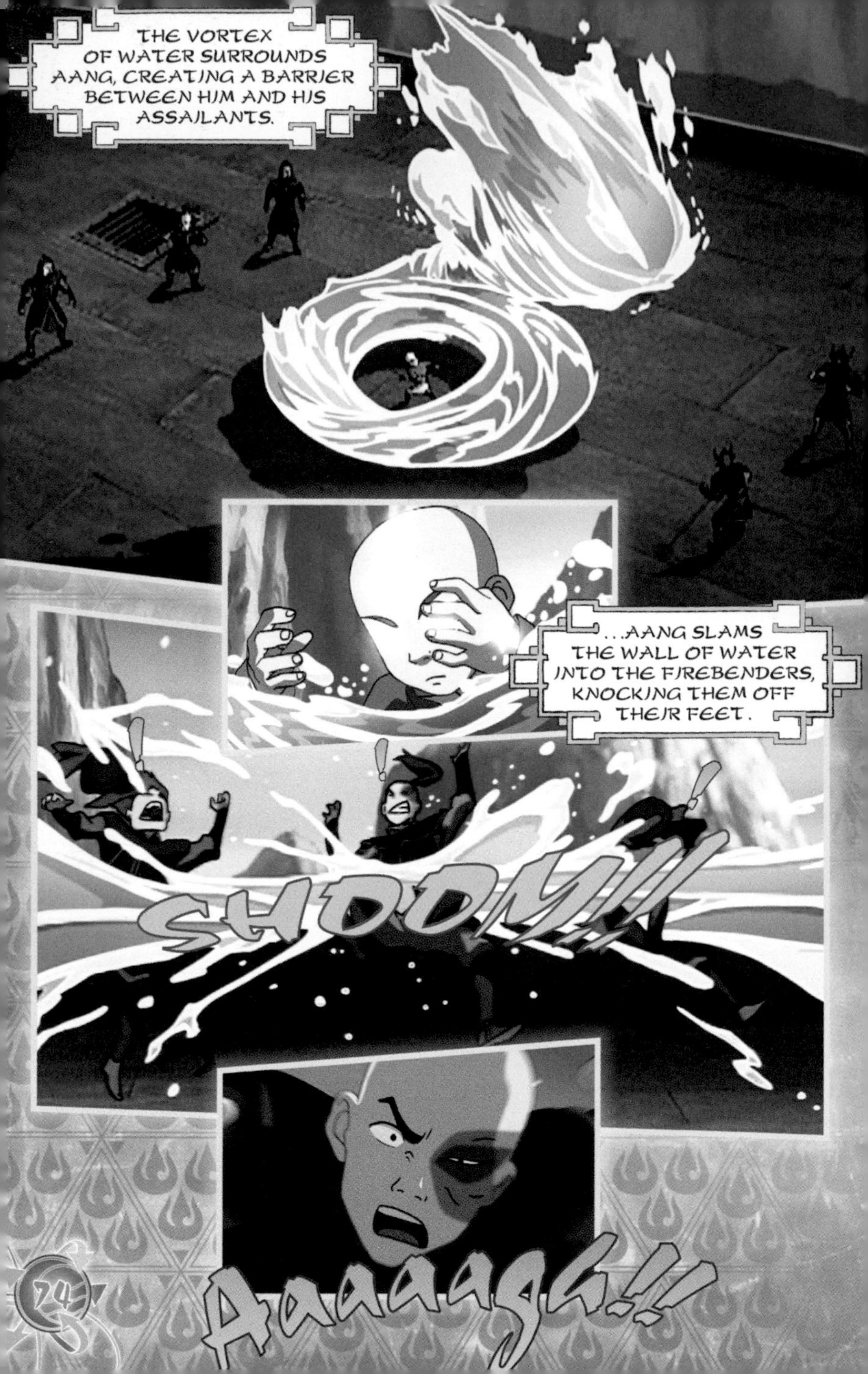
THE VORTEX OF WATER SURROUNDS AANG, CREATING A BARRIER BETWEEN HIM AND HIS ASSAILANTS.
...AANG SLAMS THE WALL OF WATER INTO THE FIREBENDERS, KNOCKING THEM OFF THEIR FEET.
!
!
!
SHOOM!!
Aaaaagh!!

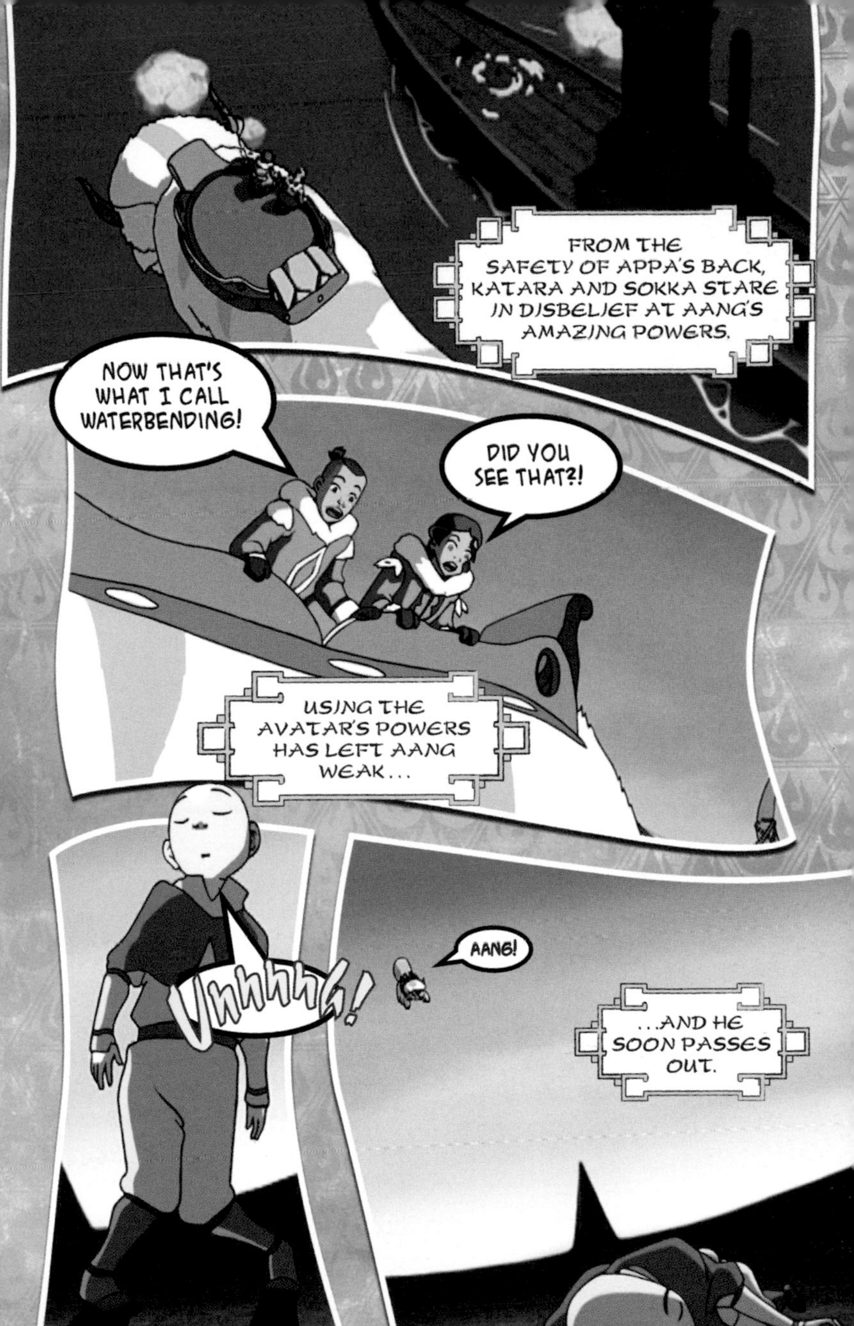
FROM THE SAFETY OF APPA'S BACK, KATARA AND SOKKA STARE IN DISBELIEF AT AANG'S AMAZING POWERS.
NOW THAT'S WHAT I CALL WATERBENDING!
DID YOU SEE THAT?!
USING THE AVATAR'S POWERS HAS LEFT AANG WEAK...
Unhhhh!
AANG!
...AND HE SOON PASSES OUT.

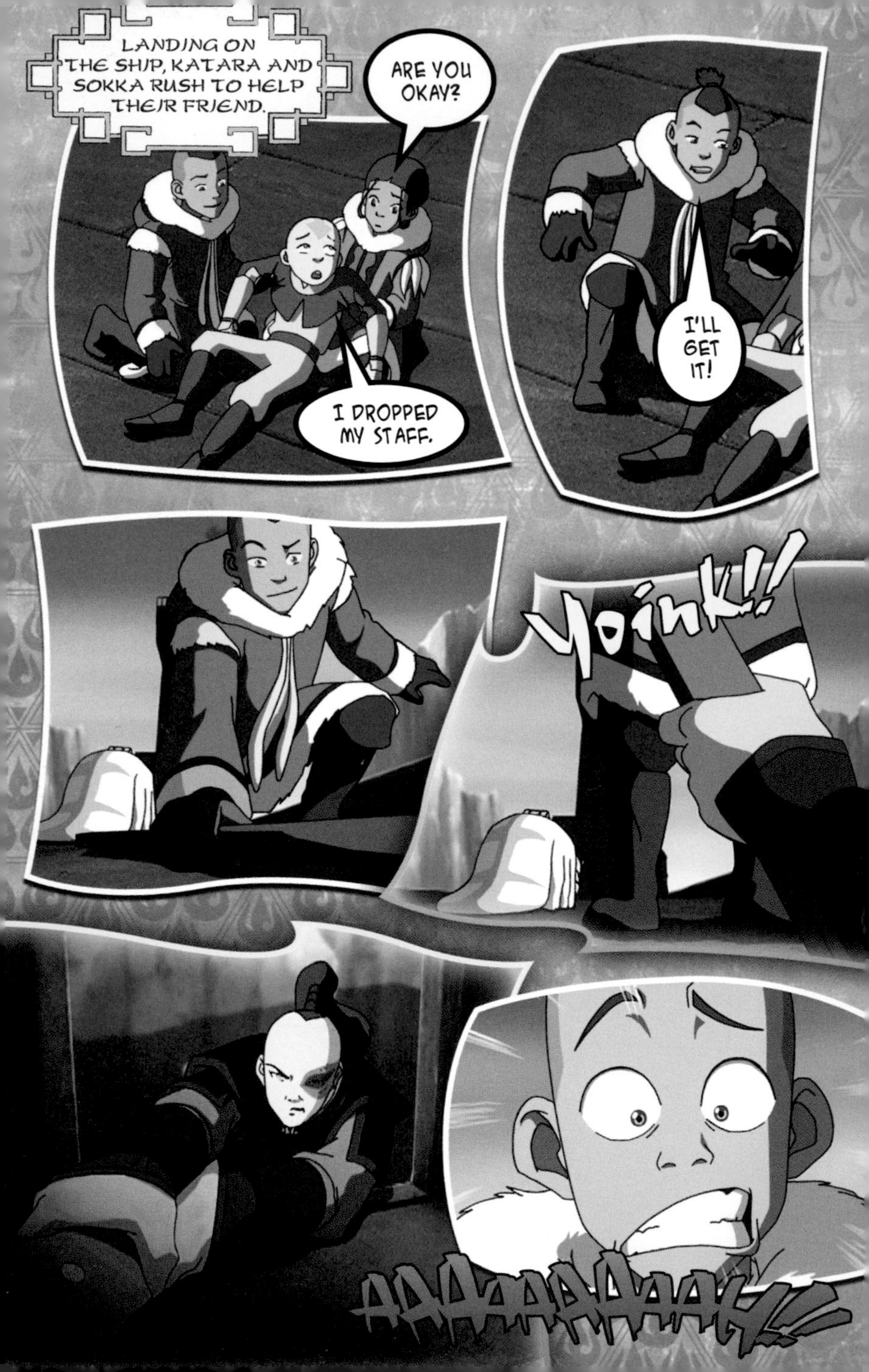
LANDING ON THE SHIP, KATARA AND SOKKA RUSH TO HELP THEIR FRIEND.
ARE YOU OKAY?
I DROPPED MY STAFF.
I'LL GET IT!
YOINK!!
AAAAAAAAAK!!

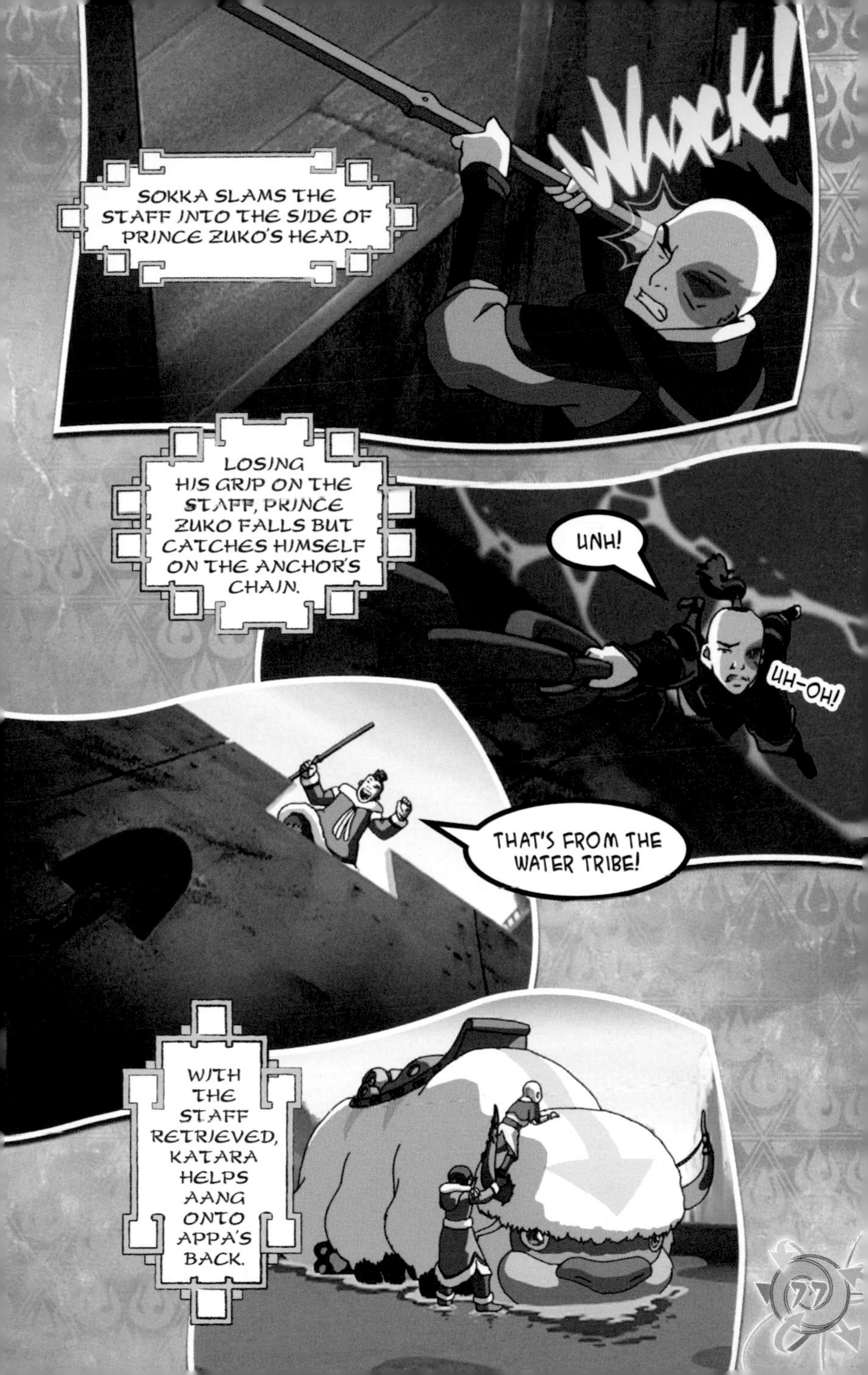
WHACK!
SOKKA SLAMS THE STAFF INTO THE SIDE OF PRINCE ZUKO'S HEAD.
LOSING HIS GRIP ON THE STAFF, PRINCE ZUKO FALLS BUT CATCHES HIMSELF ON THE ANCHOR'S CHAIN.
UNH!
UH-OH!
THAT'S FROM THE WATER TRIBE!
WITH THE STAFF RETRIEVED, KATARA HELPS AANG ONTO APPA'S BACK.

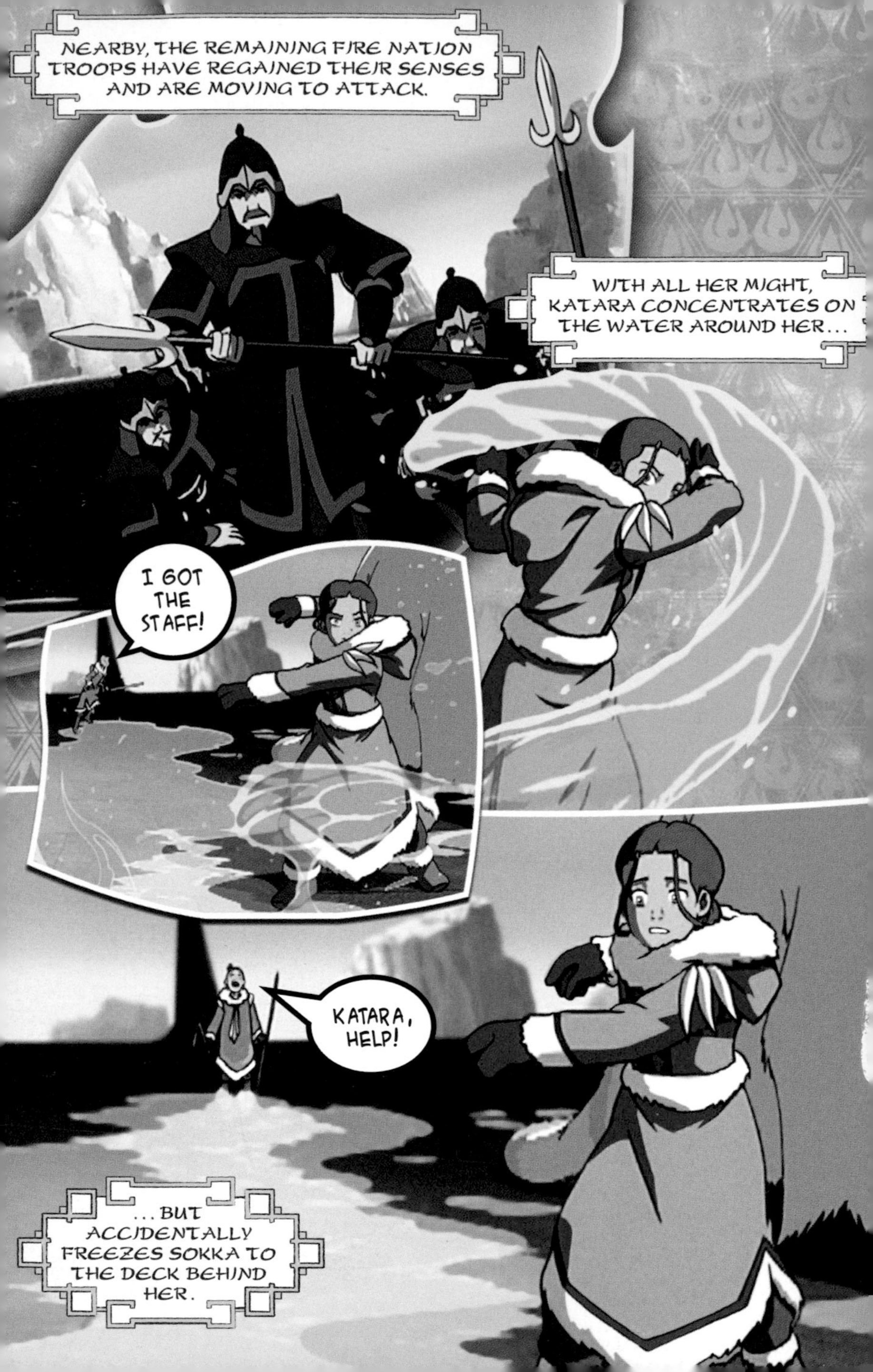
NEARBY, THE REMAINING FIRE NATION TROOPS HAVE REGAINED THEIR SENSES AND ARE MOVING TO ATTACK.
WITH ALL HER MIGHT, KATARA CONCENTRATES ON THE WATER AROUND HER...
I GOT THE STAFF!
KATARA, HELP!
...BUT ACCIDENTALLY FREEZES SOKKA TO THE DECK BEHIND HER.

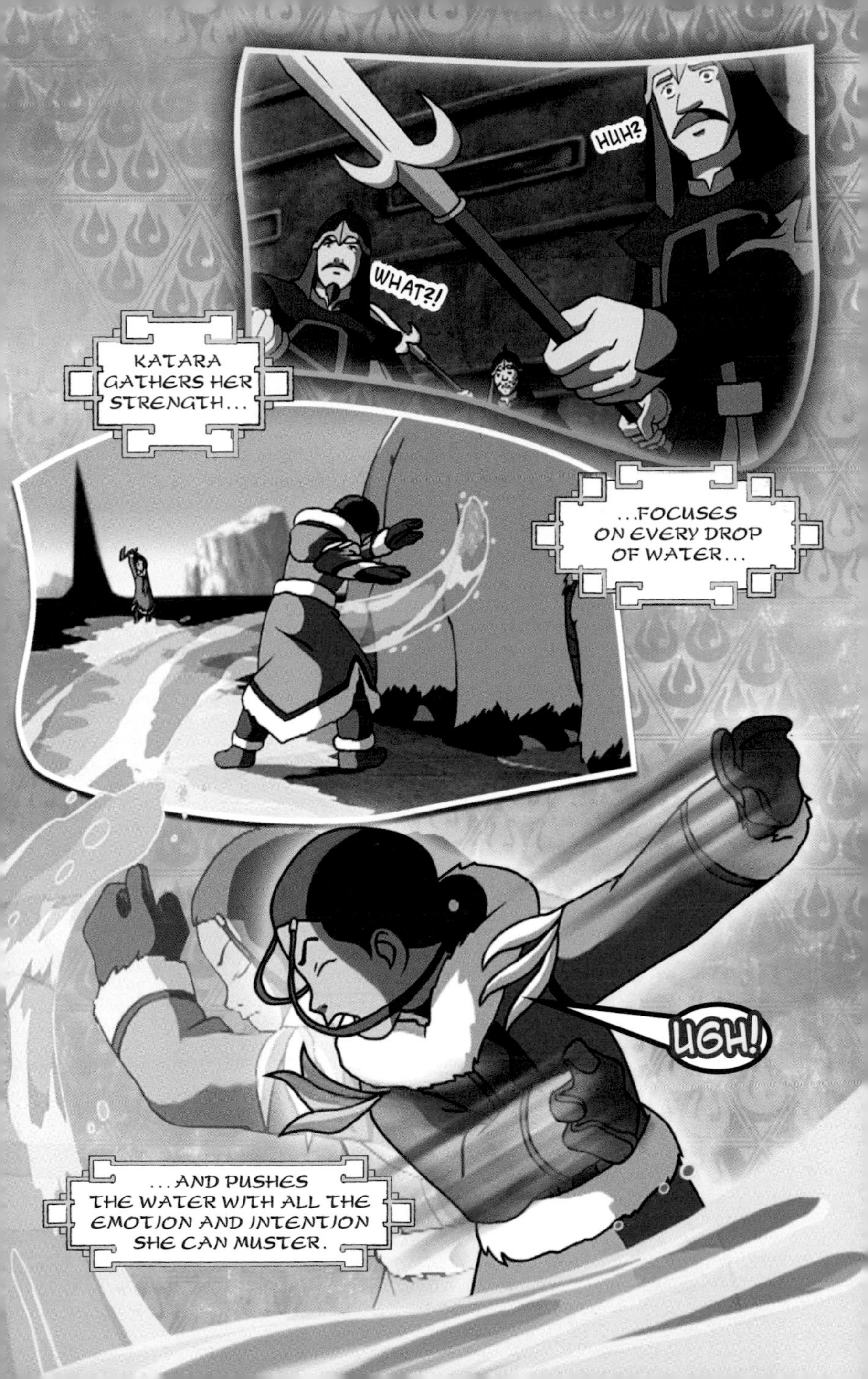
HUH?
WHAT?!
KATARA GATHERS HER STRENGTH...
...FOCUSES ON EVERY DROP OF WATER...
UGH!
...AND PUSHES THE WATER WITH ALL THE EMOTION AND INTENTION SHE CAN MUSTER.

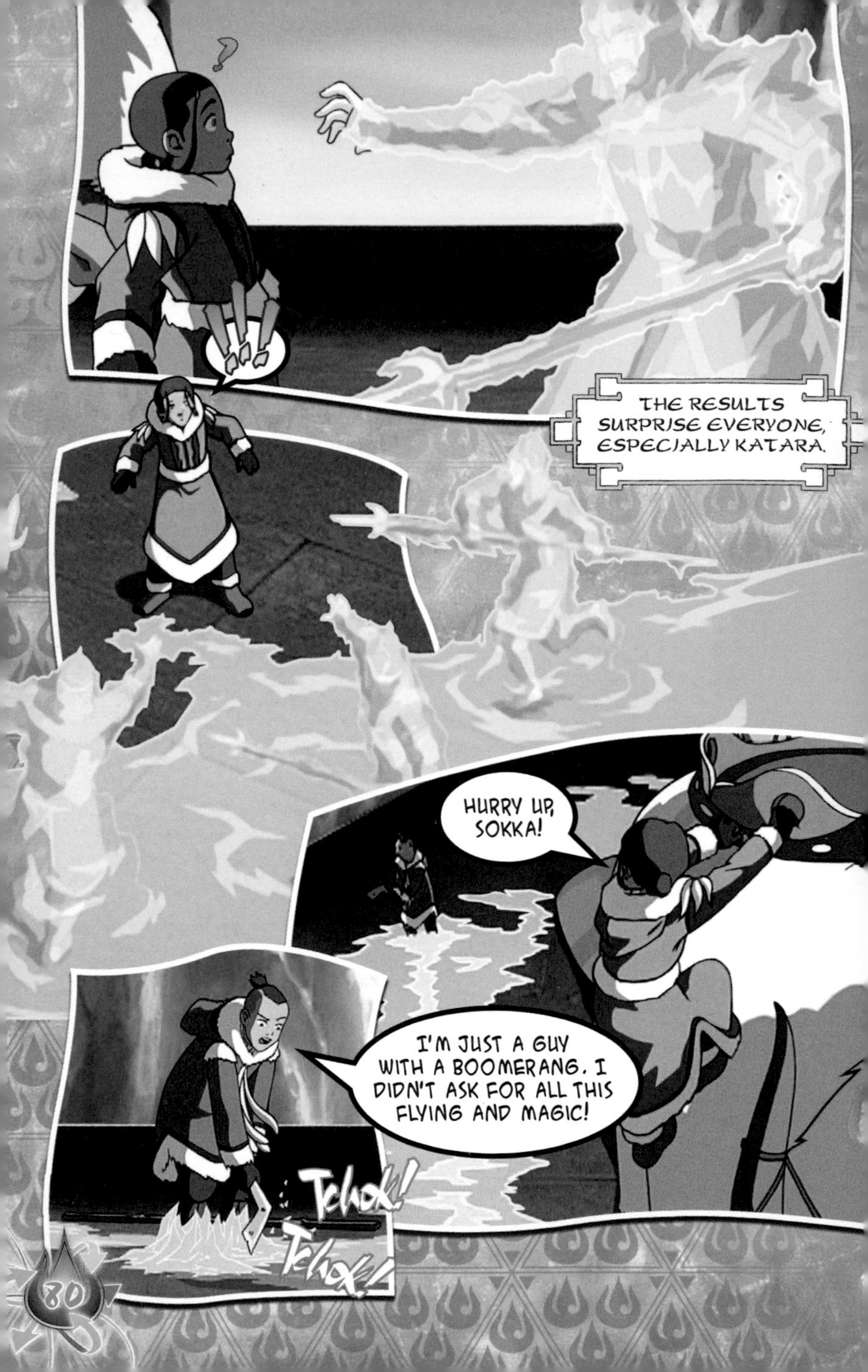
THE RESULTS SURPRISE EVERYONE, ESPECIALLY KATARA.
HURRY UP, SOKKA!
I'M JUST A GUY WITH A BOOMERANG. I DIDN'T ASK FOR ALL THIS FLYING AND MAGIC!
Tchok!
Tchok!

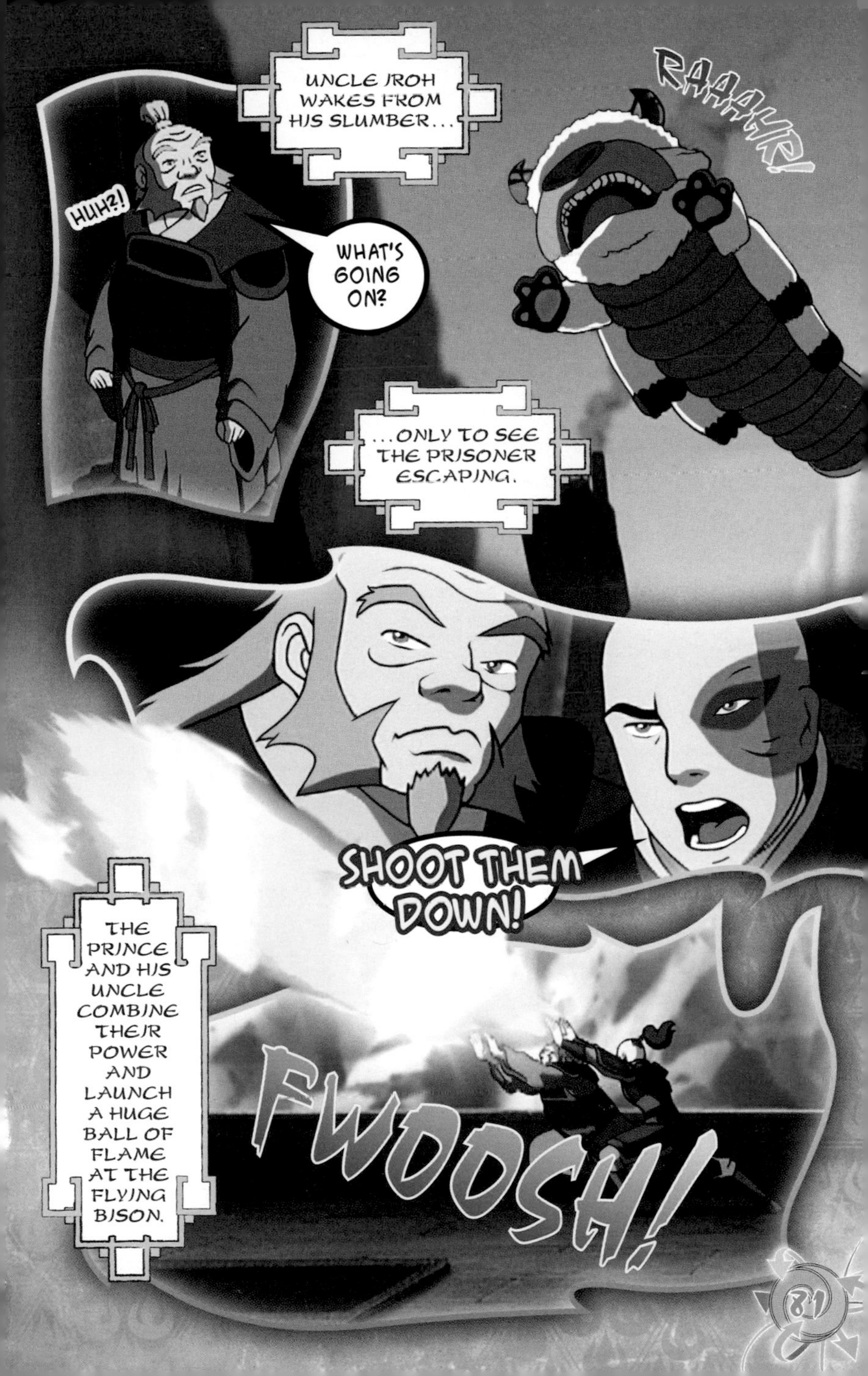

UNCLE IROH WAKES FROM HIS SLUMBER...
RAAAUR!
HUH?!
WHAT'S GOING ON?
...ONLY TO SEE THE PRISONER ESCAPING.
SHOOT THEM DOWN!
THE PRINCE AND HIS UNCLE COMBINE THEIR POWER AND LAUNCH A HUGE BALL OF FLAME AT THE FLYING BISON.
FWOOSH!

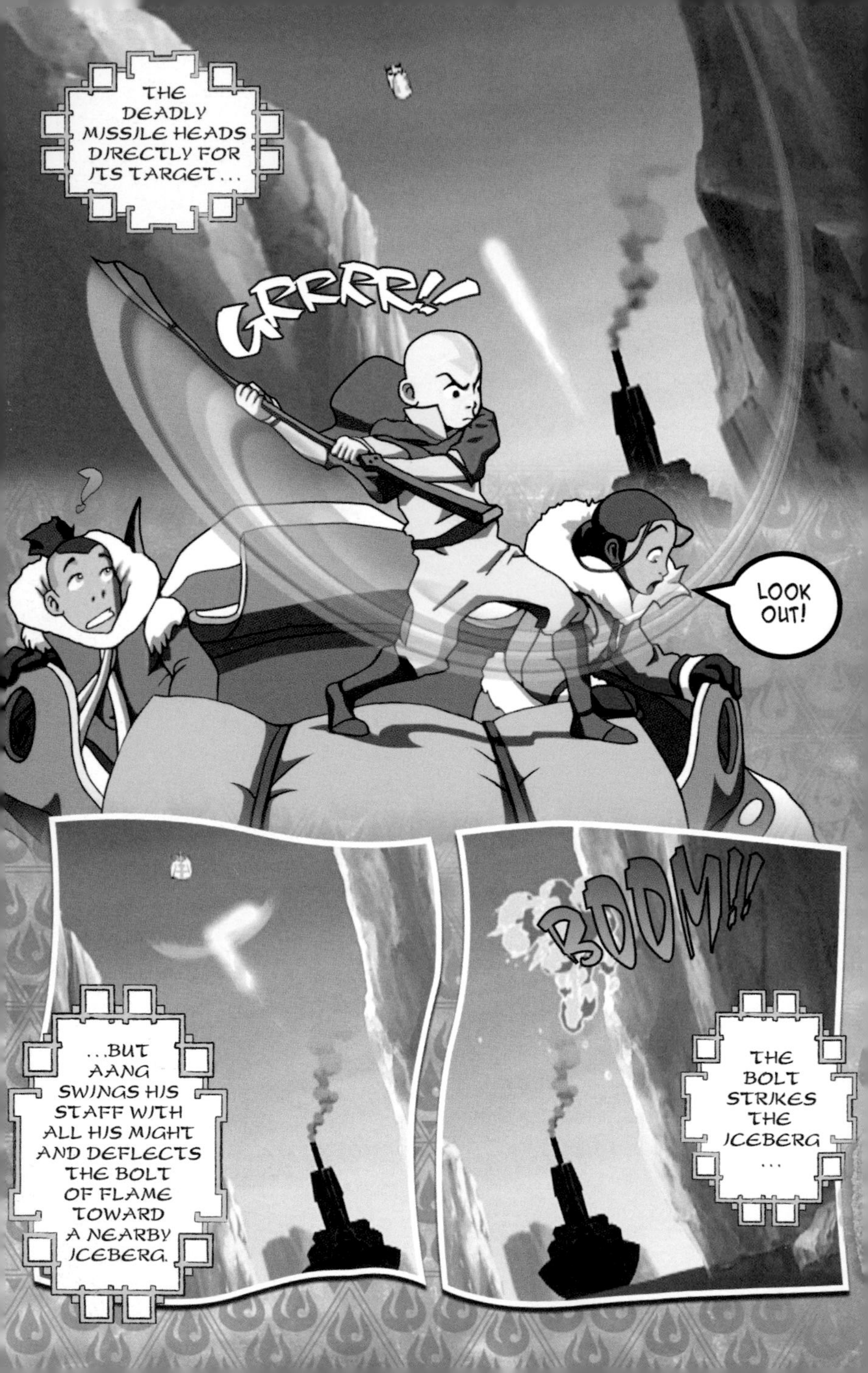
THE DEADLY MISSILE HEADS DIRECTLY FOR ITS TARGET . . .
GRRRR!!
?
LOOK OUT!
. . .BUT AANG SWINGS HIS STAFF WITH ALL HIS MIGHT AND DEFLECTS THE BOLT OF FLAME TOWARD A NEARBY ICEBERG.
BOOM!!
THE BOLT STRIKES THE ICEBERG . . .

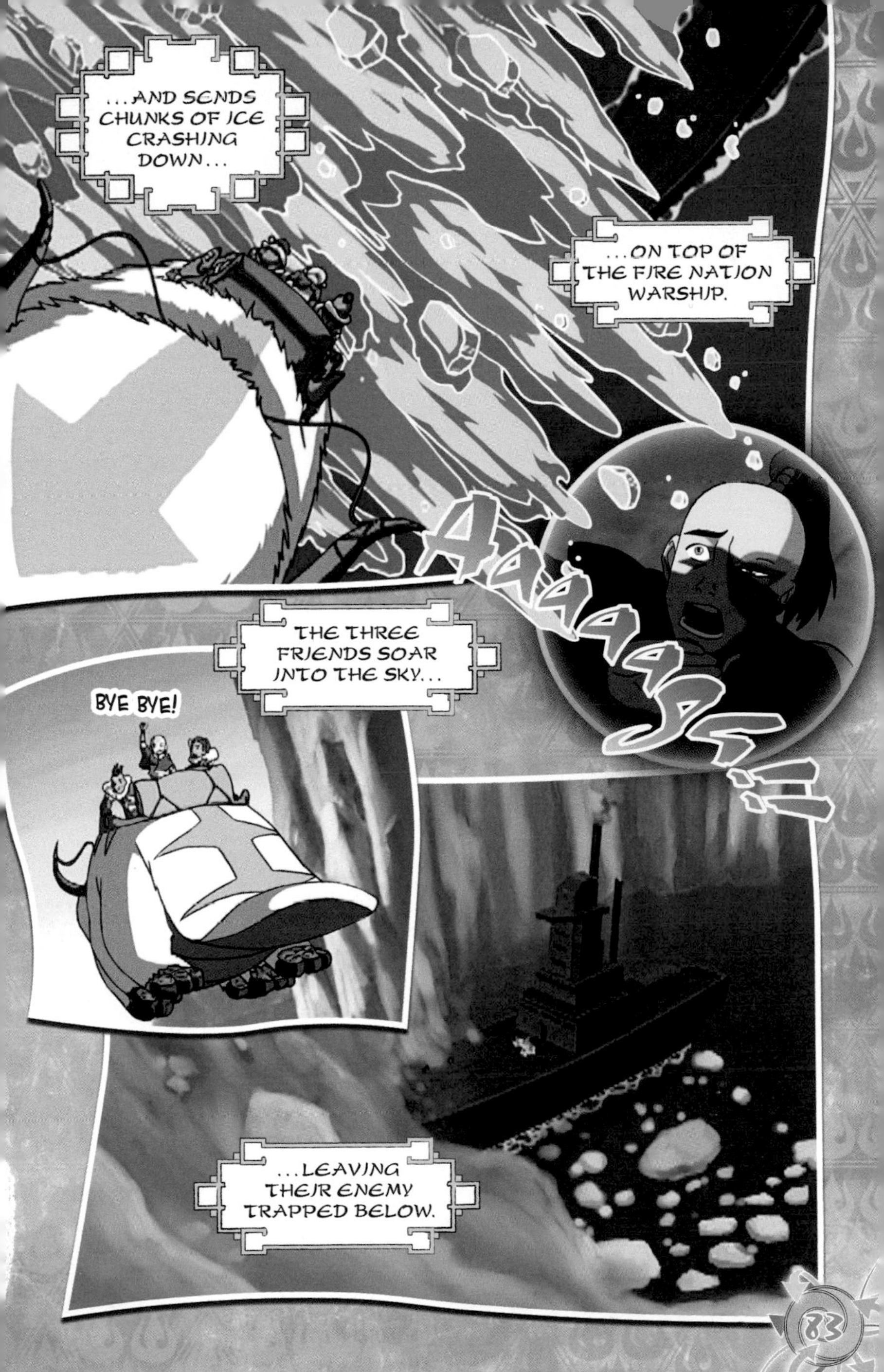

...AND SENDS CHUNKS OF ICE CRASHING DOWN...
...ON TOP OF THE FIRE NATION WARSHIP.
AAAAAAGG!!!
THE THREE FRIENDS SOAR INTO THE SKY...
BYE BYE!
...LEAVING THEIR ENEMY TRAPPED BELOW.

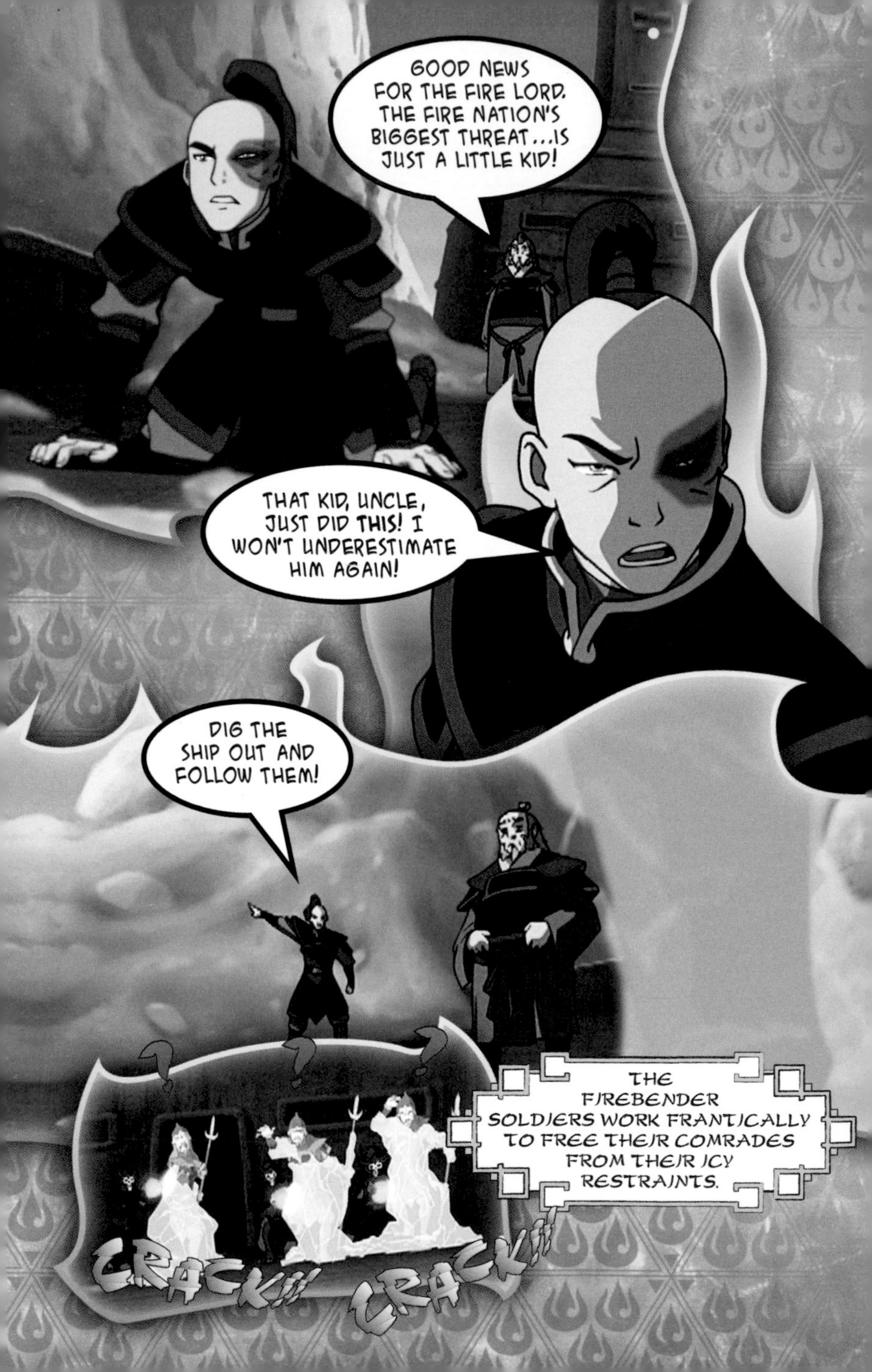
GOOD NEWS FOR THE FIRE LORD. THE FIRE NATION'S BIGGEST THREAT...IS JUST A LITTLE KID!
THAT KID, UNCLE, JUST DID THIS! I WON'T UNDERESTIMATE HIM AGAIN!
DIG THE SHIP OUT AND FOLLOW THEM!
THE FIREBENDER SOLDIERS WORK FRANTICALLY TO FREE THEIR COMRADES FROM THEIR ICY RESTRAINTS.
CRACK!!
CRACK!!

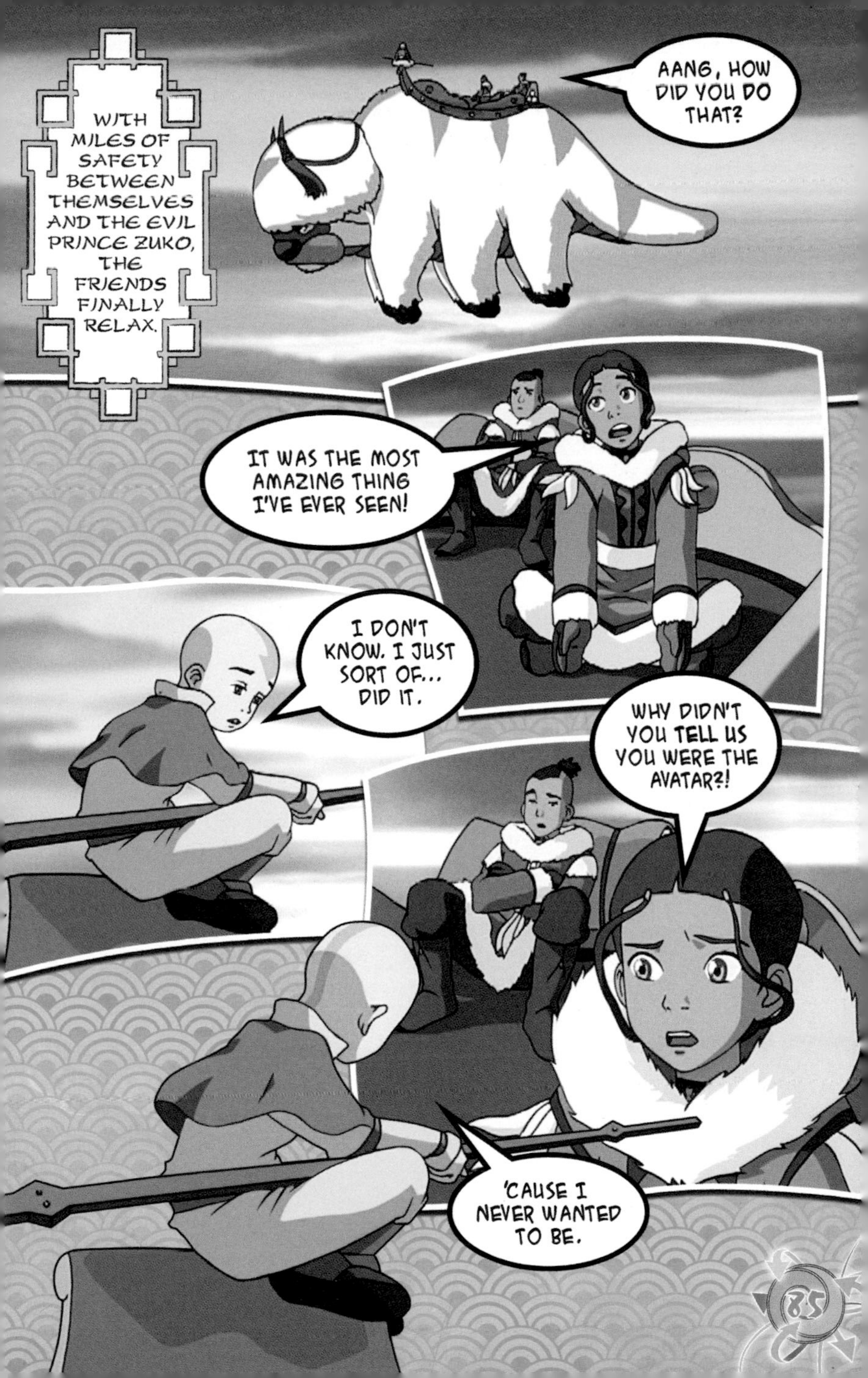
WITH MILES OF SAFETY BETWEEN THEMSELVES AND THE EVIL PRINCE ZUKO, THE FRIENDS FINALLY RELAX.
AANG, HOW DID YOU DO THAT?
IT WAS THE MOST AMAZING THING I'VE EVER SEEN!
I DON'T KNOW. I JUST SORT OF... DID IT.
WHY DIDN'T YOU TELL US YOU WERE THE AVATAR?!
'CAUSE I NEVER WANTED TO BE.

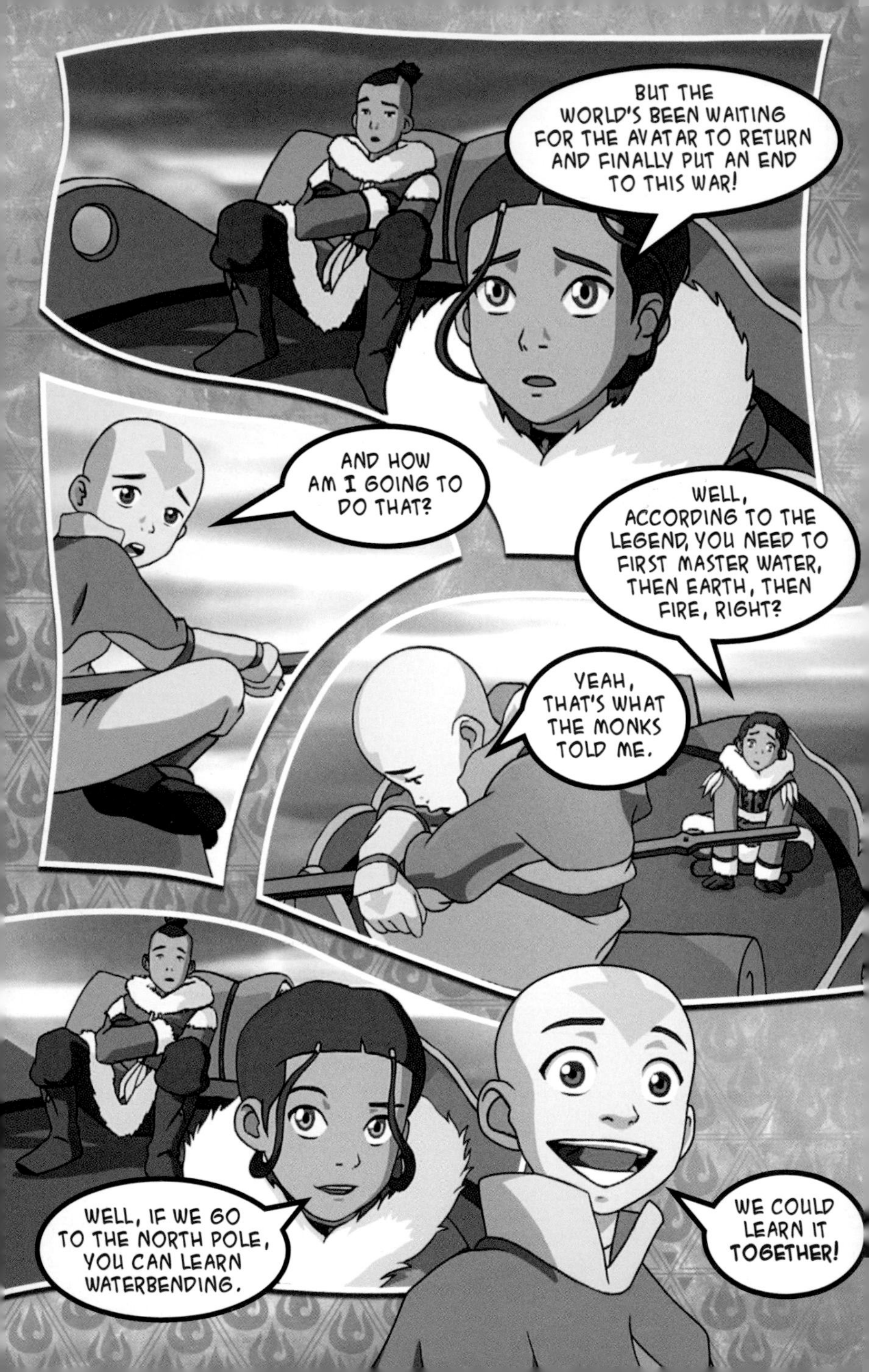
BUT THE WORLD'S BEEN WAITING FOR THE AVATAR TO RETURN AND FINALLY PUT AN END TO THIS WAR!
AND HOW AM I GOING TO DO THAT?
WELL, ACCORDING TO THE LEGEND, YOU NEED TO FIRST MASTER WATER, THEN EARTH, THEN FIRE, RIGHT?
YEAH, THAT'S WHAT THE MONKS TOLD ME.
WELL, IF WE GO TO THE NORTH POLE, YOU CAN LEARN WATERBENDING.
WE COULD LEARN IT TOGETHER!

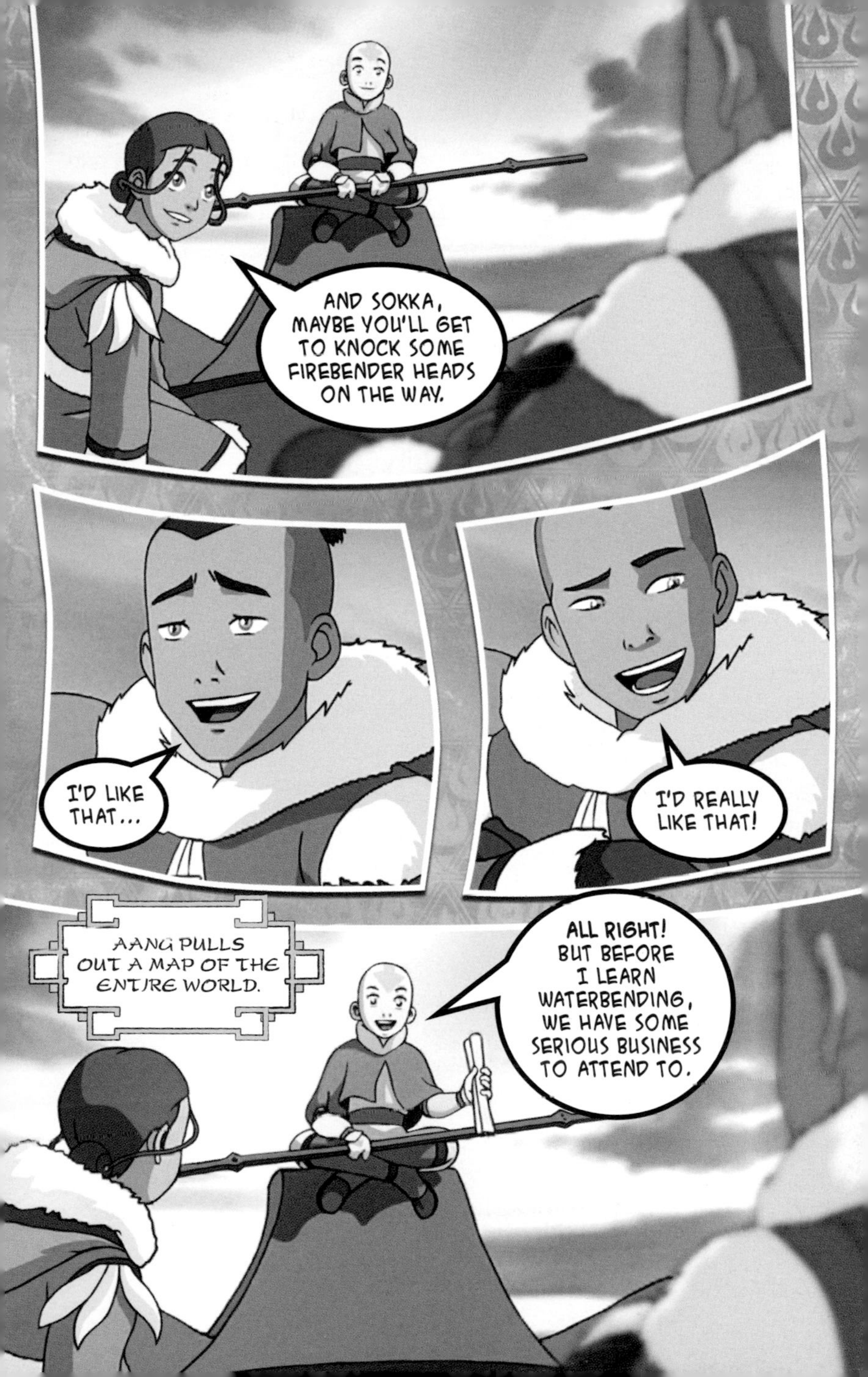
AND SOKKA, MAYBE YOU'LL GET TO KNOCK SOME FIREBENDER HEADS ON THE WAY.
I'D LIKE THAT...
I'D REALLY LIKE THAT!
AANG PULLS OUT A MAP OF THE ENTIRE WORLD.
ALL RIGHT! BUT BEFORE I LEARN WATERBENDING, WE HAVE SOME SERIOUS BUSINESS TO ATTEND TO.

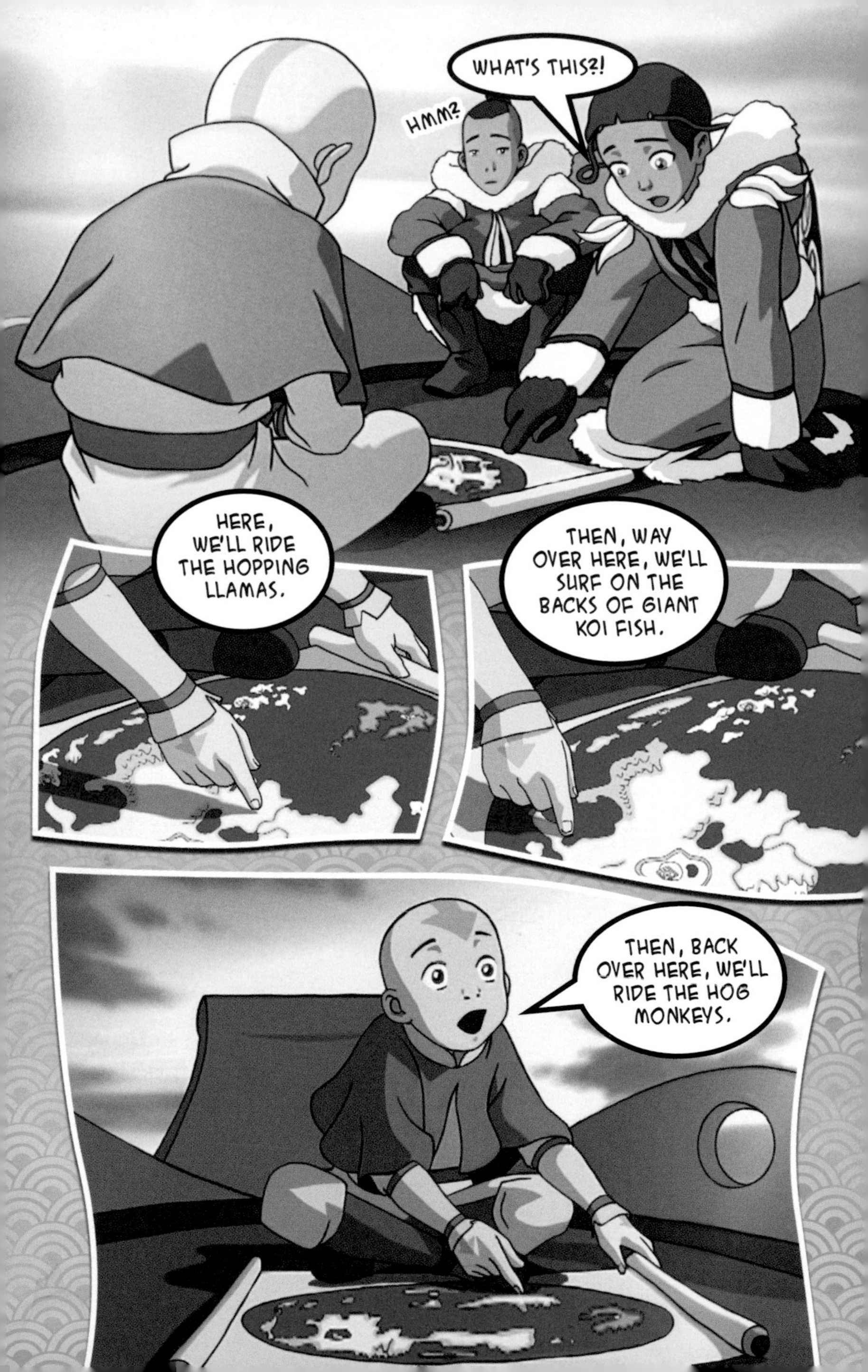
WHAT'S THIS?!
HMM?
HERE, WE'LL RIDE THE HOPPING LLAMAS.
THEN, WAY OVER HERE, WE'LL SURF ON THE BACKS OF GIANT KOI FISH.
THEN, BACK OVER HERE, WE'LL RIDE THE HOG MONKEYS.

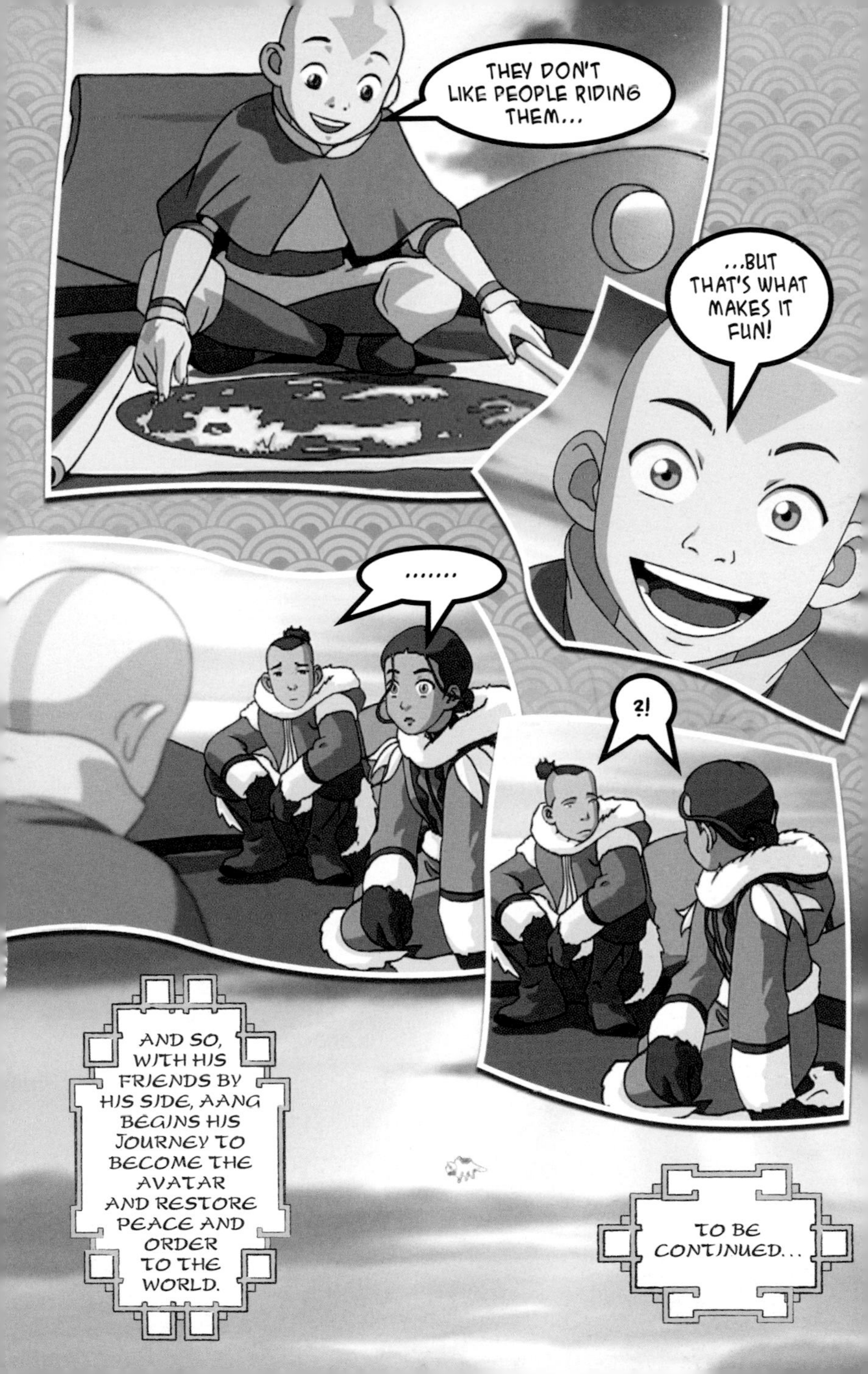
THEY DON'T LIKE PEOPLE RIDING THEM...
...BUT THAT'S WHAT MAKES IT FUN!
....
?!
AND SO, WITH HIS FRIENDS BY HIS SIDE, AANG BEGINS HIS JOURNEY TO BECOME THE AVATAR AND RESTORE PEACE AND ORDER TO THE WORLD.
TO BE CONTINUED...

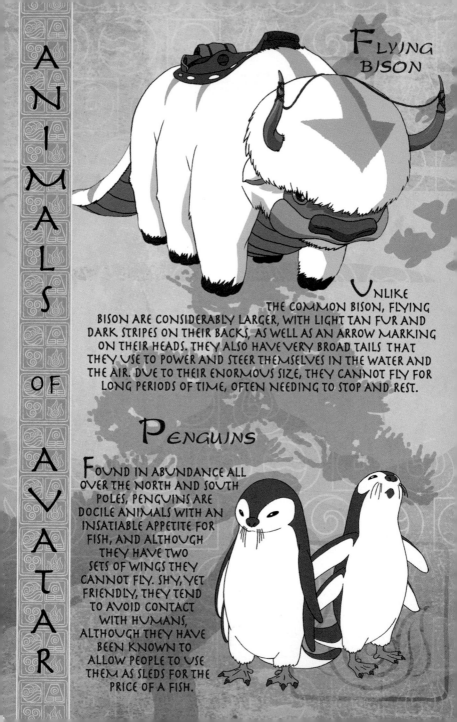

Animals of Avatar

Flying Bison

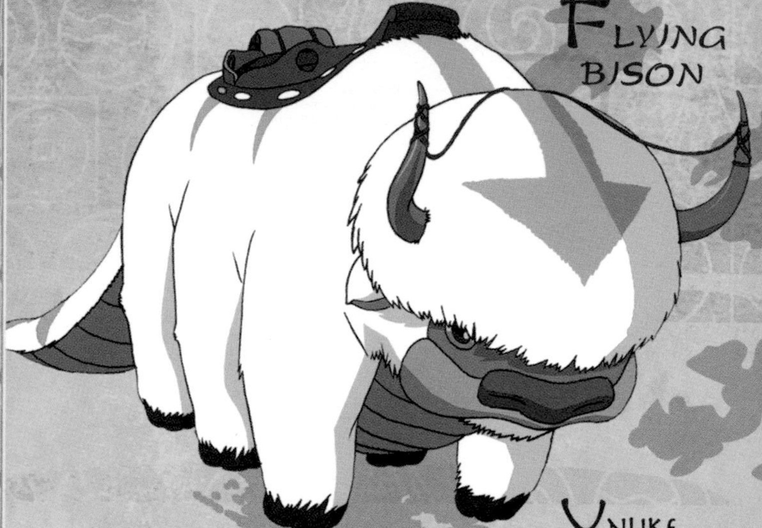

Unlike the common bison, flying bison are considerably larger, with light tan fur and dark stripes on their backs, as well as an arrow marking on their heads. They also have very broad tails that they use to power and steer themselves in the water and the air. Due to their enormous size, they cannot fly for long periods of time, often needing to stop and rest.

Penguins

Found in abundance all over the North and South Poles, penguins are docile animals with an insatiable appetite for fish, and although they have two sets of wings they cannot fly. Shy, yet friendly, they tend to avoid contact with humans, although they have been known to allow people to use them as sleds for the price of a fish.

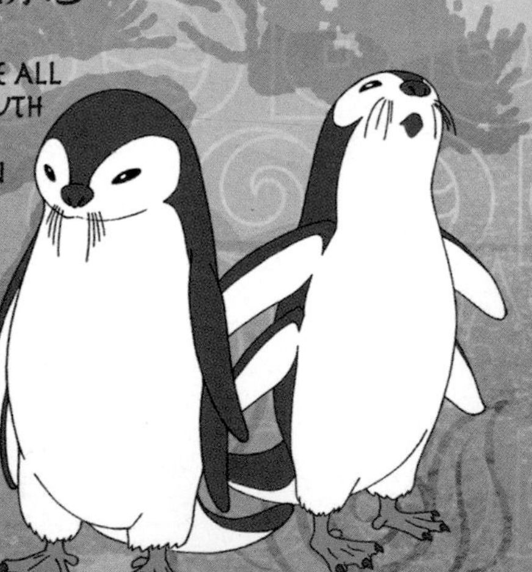

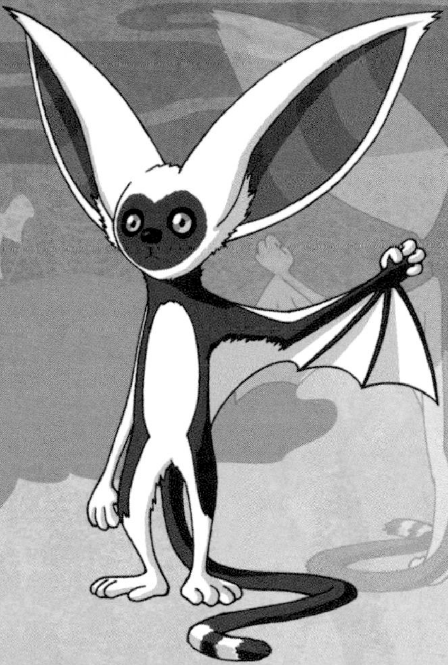

Winged Lemurs

Looking like a cross between a spotted bat and a black and white lemur, these creatures are extremely intelligent and have highly developed senses of hearing and smell. They can be trained, but if there is food nearby, they will eat it, even if they are told not to. Winged lemurs are nervous creatures; they panic easily and will screech in fear if they feel threatened.

Zebra Seals

Zebra seals get their name from the distinctive striping on their backs, which they use to camouflage their numbers from predators while swimming or hunting for fish. Zebra seals live together in small groups and avoid contact with other animals whenever possible.

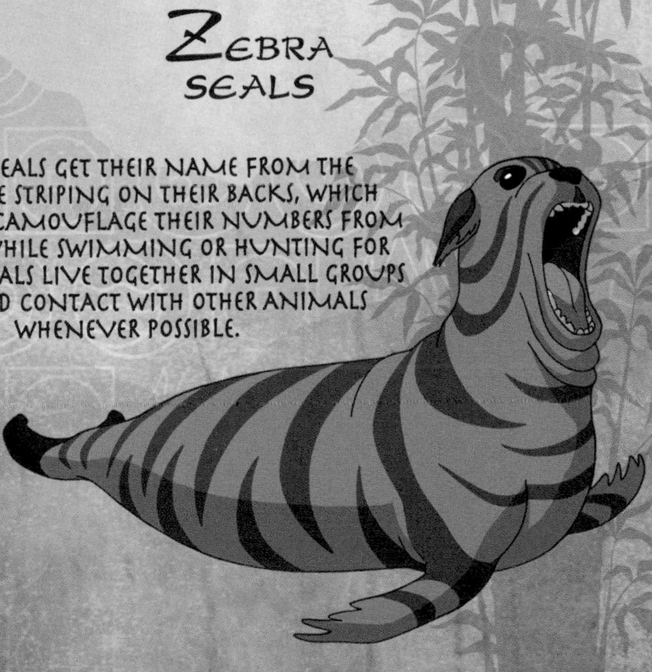

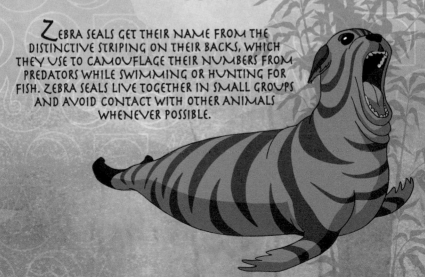

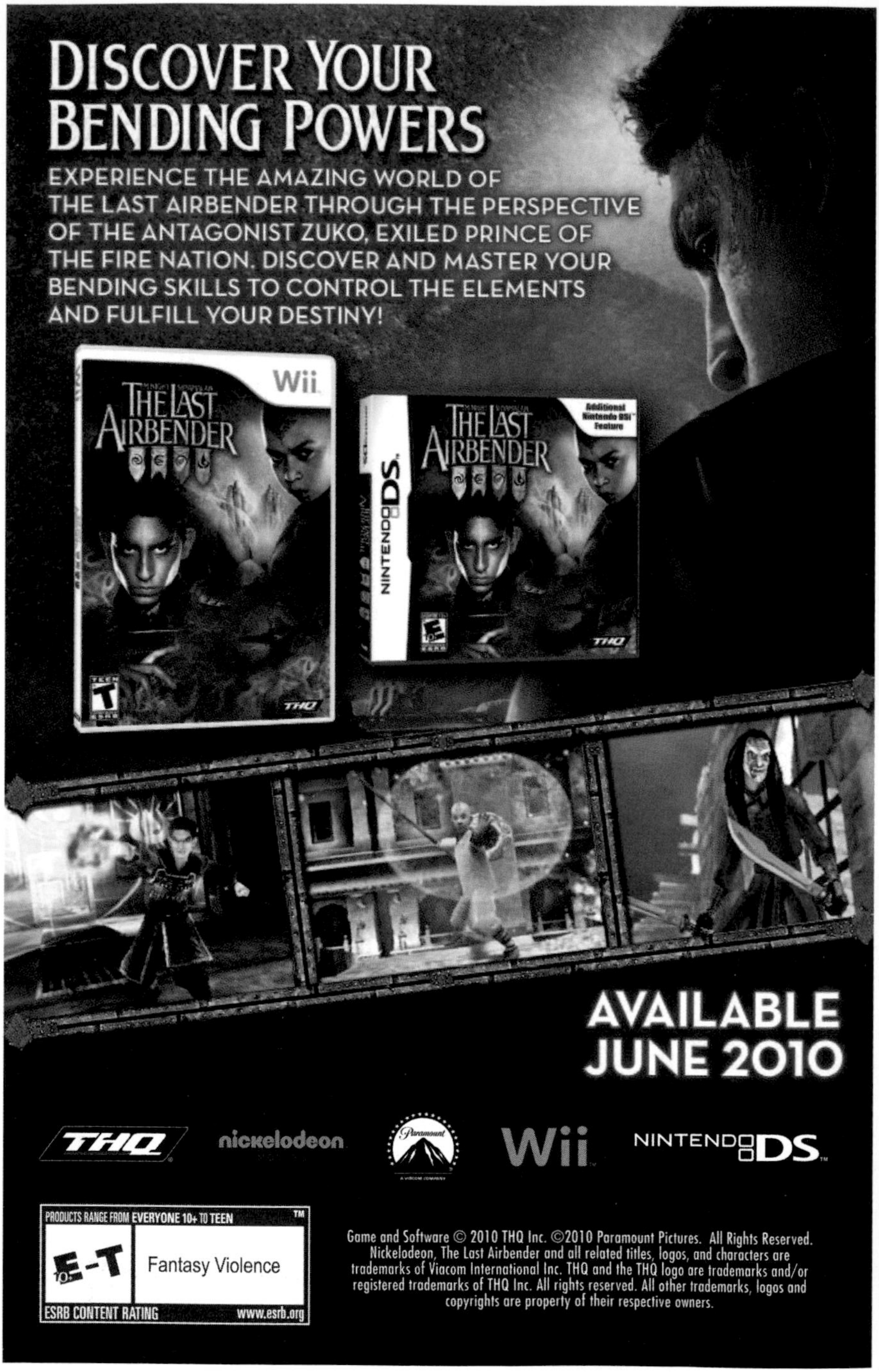
DISCOVER YOUR
BENDING POWERS
EXPERIENCE THE AMAZING WORLD OF THE LAST AIRBENDER THROUGH THE PERSPECTIVE OF THE ANTAGONIST ZUKO, EXILED PRINCE OF THE FIRE NATION. DISCOVER AND MASTER YOUR BENDING SKILLS TO CONTROL THE ELEMENTS AND FULFILL YOUR DESTINY!
Wii
THE LAST AIRBENDER
NINTENDO DS
Additional Nintendo DSi Feature
AVAILABLE
JUNE 2010
PRODUCTS RANGE FROM EVERYONE 10+ TO TEEN
Fantasy Violence
ESRB CONTENT RATING www.esrb.org
Game and Software © 2010 THQ Inc. ©2010 Paramount Pictures. All Rights Reserved. Nickelodeon, The Last Airbender and all related titles, logos, and characters are trademarks of Viacom International Inc. THQ and the THQ logo are trademarks and/or registered trademarks of THQ Inc. All rights reserved. All other trademarks, logos and copyrights are property of their respective owners.

THE OFFICIAL GRAPHIC NOVELS OF THE BLOCKBUSTER FILM

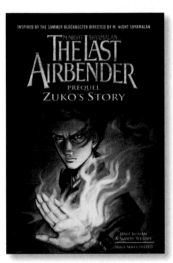

THE LAST AIRBENDER: PREQUEL: ZUKO'S STORY

WRITTEN BY DAVE ROMAN AND ALISON WILGUS
ILLUSTRATED BY NINA MATSUMOTO

Banished from the Fire Nation, Prince Zuko's only chance at redemption lies in finding the mystical Avatar who once kept the four nations in balance.

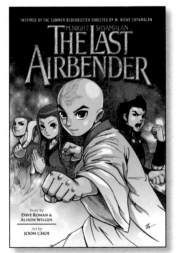

THE LAST AIRBENDER

WRITTEN BY DAVE ROMAN AND ALISON WILGUS
ILLUSTRATED BY JOON CHOI

It is Aang's destiny as the Avatar to bring balance to the world. But will even the powers of the last of the airbenders be enough to challenge the ruthless Fire Nation?

WWW.DELREYMANGA.COM

SHUGO CHARA!

PEACH-PIT

CREATORS OF *DEARS* AND *ROZEN MAIDEN*

PEACH-PIT
CREATORS OF DEARS AND ROZEN MAIDEN
SHUGO CHARA!
1

Everybody at Seiyo Elementary thinks that stylish and supercool Amu has it all. But nobody knows the real Amu, a shy girl who wishes she had the courage to truly be herself. Changing Amu's life is going to take more than wishes and dreams—it's going to take a little magic! One morning, Amu finds a surprise in her bed: three strange little eggs. Each egg contains a Guardian Character, an angel-like being who can give her the power to be someone new. With the help of her Guardian Characters, Amu is about to discover that her true self is even more amazing than she ever dreamed.

Special extras in each volume! Read them all!

VISIT WWW.DELREYMANGA.COM TO:

- **Read sample pages**
- **Sign up for Del Rey's free manga e-newsletter**
- **Find out the latest about new Del Rey Manga series**

DEL REY MANGA デルレイ

The Otaku's Choice™

Fairy Navigator Runa

STORY BY MIYOKO IKEDA
ILLUSTRATIONS BY MICHIYO KIKUTA

1
Fairy Navigator Runa
story by Miyoko Ikeda
illustrations by Michiyo Kikuta

THE LEGENDARY CHILD

As a baby, Runa Rindō was left in front of a school for foster children, wearing a mysterious pendant. Now she's in fourth grade and strange things are starting to happen around her. It's only a matter of time before she discovers her secret powers—and her quest as the Legendary Fairy Child begins!

From the illustrator of *Mamotte! Lollipop*

Special extras in each volume! Read them all!

VISIT WWW.DELREYMANGA.COM TO:

- **Read sample pages**
- **Sign up for Del Rey's free manga e-newsletter**
- **Find out the latest about new Del Rey Manga series**

DEL REY MANGA デルレイ
The Otaku's Choice™